Defining Moments

Relationships, Rebellion and Redemption

Jeffrey Pipes Guice

©2020 All rights reserved. This book or any portion thereof may not be reproduced or used in any manner whatsoever without the express written permission of the publisher except for the use of brief quotations in a book review.

Print ISBN: 978-1-09833-753-7

eBook ISBN: 978-1-09833-754-4

Preface

While I always wanted to compile a collection of poems and short stories, it really started when COVID-19 completely changed my every day routine, I decided to beat what I called my COVID-19 blues by shifting my focus to do something positive.

In my quest to push myself in a completely different direction, I decided to write my first book of poems and short stories. I'm calling this book "Defining Moments: Relationships, Rebellion and Redemption" as a way to identify various sides of my personality and understand who I was, who I am and who I want to be as a friend, a father and a normal human being. I realize that "normal" means different things to different people, but I hope that whoever reads this book will find at least one poem in one of the nine chapters that will make them laugh, or cry, or connect on some kind of normal human level.

I want Defining Moments to tell a story, sometimes real and sometimes fictional, about my peculiar view of the eccentric world around me, the people, places and things that shape my different way of thinking.

Most of these poems or short stories started with a thought or an image. I describe my writing approach as "method writing" whereby I immerse myself into a visual and imagine what the person or place depicted might be thinking. Whether it's a little boy or a girl, a desolate street in the French Quarter, or a totally bizarre visual, I go deeper within, allowing my imagination to completely take over.

When writing a short story or a prayer, I find I can transcend my ego, and allow the words or thoughts to write themselves.

I feel it's important to share with my readers that in 2020 I am celebrating my twelfth year of sobriety. It's only been in the last few years that I have finally come to understand myself, including my shortcomings and insecurities, which has helped me to reach this point where I feel strong enough to write this book. It's important to also point out the fact that during this time I've come to realize that I no longer need 5,000 Facebook friends in my life, but only the handful of people who are indeed closest to me who are the ones that have helped me find my comfort level to write this book. I can't describe the depth of love and friendship that I have received from these people, which include my parents, Anne and Jerry, my friends, Bill and Jane, and my three beautiful children, Juliette, Pipes and Gus. I love you all!

Again, this is only my first book and I hope each of you find at least one poem, or short story, or even a prayer to which you can relate.

I want to confess that I still have not arrived at the answer to my question, which is how many poems does one have to write before they can consider themself an actual poet? I guess it's up to the readers to decide. Enjoy!

Jeffrey Pipes Guice

New Orleans, LA

Chapters

Chapter 1: True Love, Near Misses and Friendship 1

Chapter 2: Mardi Gras 28

Chapter 3: New Orleans History 48

Chapter 4: Humor and Limericks 66

Chapter 5: Society and Politics 88

Chapter 6: The Dark Side 108

Chapter 7: Self Reflection 128

Chapter 8: Cemetery Reflections 145

Chapter 9: Spirituality and My Relationship
With My Higher Power 164

Chapter 1:
True Love, Near Misses and Friendship

The Apple Of My Eye

Every time I think of you my hands began to shake.
My knees begin to wobble and my head begins to ache.
You caused me nothing but trouble and I often wondered why.
I was good to you and I loved you so. You were the apple of my eye.

It started on the afternoon of the 23rd of May.
You were dating a boy named Anderson
but your game he couldn't play.
Then when you saw me you fell in love
and you still love me today.
But I knew we couldn't make it work
and this is all I have to say.

Every time I think of you my hands begin shake.
My knees being to wobble and my head begins to ache.
You caused me nothing but trouble and I often wondered why.
I was good to you and I loved you so. You were the apple of my eye.

When I first saw your smile, I had to kiss your lips.
It was a fairytale love at first sight.
I nibbled on your ears and I hickied on your neck
as you wiggled in girlish delight.
Then Anderson showed up with his football team
and he challenged me to a fight.
I got some good licks in and I broke a guy's nose
as they ran off into the night.

Every time I think of you my hands begin shake.
My knees being to wobble and my head begins to ache.
You caused me nothing but trouble and I often wondered why.
I was good to you and I loved you so. You were the apple of my eye.

When your momma found out, she put a stop to our lovin'
and it broke my heart to bits.
Your daddy was a judge and when your momma told 'em 'bout our lovin'
it threw him into fits.
And the very next day the word got to me
that our lovin' days were pretty much done.
If I ever showed up again around the judge's big house
I'd be facing the end of his gun.

Every time I think of you my hands begin to shake.
My knees begin to wobble and my head begins to ache.
You caused me nothing but trouble and I often wondered why.
I was good to you and I loved you so. You were the apple of my eye.

It was few years later when our paths were to cross
and you invited me home for a spin.
You took care of my business and when we were through
I left you wearing nothin' more than a grin.
You loved me early on, and you loved me that night
and you still love me today.
But I knew we couldn't make it work
and this is all I have to say.

Every time I think of you my hands begin shake.
My knees begin to wobble and my head begins to ache.
You caused me nothing but trouble and I often wondered why.
I was good to you and I loved you so. You were the apple of my eye.

Come Bite The Apple

It started completely innocent
With all the best of intentions...
We were both working really hard
On our mutual abstentions...

We went together as friends
To her first Mardi Gras ball...
The furthest thing from my mind
Was that I was going to quickly fall...

Our friendship was a gift
From our Higher Power up above...
It wasn't suppose to happen
That I would somehow fall in love...

My sweet blue-eyed Eve
I completely missed the riddle...
You deserve all the credit
For playing me like an old fiddle...

Your juicy luscious lips kept saying
"Come bite the apple for a while."
After all your many empty coos
I fell victim to your measured guile...

You didn't mean to be cruel
But I guess it's all the same...
You played me like a bloomin' fool
That's how we players play the game...

I now know you didn't feel a connection
It was all just a one way thing...
I fell in love with you, my Eve
Not realizing I was just a fling...

My sweet blue-eyed Eve
Played me like a shiny toy...
I allowed my heart to get broken
Just like a young giddy school boy...

Why couldn't I just see it
I tried to teach you how to fight...
But I offer you no blame
For my broken heart tonight...

For once under your spell
I lost my plan of flight...
And in the midst of all my pain
I finally saw the light...

While deep in solemn prayer
The answer fell into my lap...
For you, my sweet blue-eyed Eve
Became my thinking trap...

So my sweet blue-eyed Eve
Just give me the heave-ho shove...
You've been playing with me long enough
I'm just not the one you'll ever love...

Image: Takahiko Mori

My Southern Magnolia

"What's in a name?" Juliet asks Romeo...
"That which we call a rose by any other name would smell as sweet..."
My Southern Magnolia is nothing like a thorny rose...
Her blossoms are of a breathtaking treat...

Her beauty and splendor often attract all the others...
Her fragrant blossoms last through the Spring and Summer...
There's no ending of love for my Southern Magnolia...
While constantly battling the curious newcomer...

Her lemon and vanilla fragrance are of a Southern nectar...
It's her velvet skin I caress with quiet detail...
As she presses her soft body against mine...
Her extended limbs are sturdy, yet frail...

As I trace her beautiful blossom...
She gently purrs as if she's having a thrilla...
It's then when I taste her sweet Southern nectar...
With her soft hints of lemon and vanilla...

I love my Southern Magnolia...
With all her beauty, sweet smell and grace...
It's hard to imagine a life without her...
She's in my heart, my thoughts and my embrace...

Two Sides To Every Story

Beware of the soft illusions...
While you're listening to her voice...
It might not be what it all seems...
Beware of making the wrong first choice...

There are two sides to every story...
And sometimes three or four...
But when the story stops adding up...
One must find the nearest door...
Our friends will try to warn us...
Beware of people, places and things...
You might think twice about her...
The pain and suffering that she brings...
But when I looked into her eyes...
All I saw was a beautiful face...
Absent were the warning flags...
I was in awe of her childish grace...

When I look back upon it today...
I smile slyly in my mind...
Even though she stole my heart...
She made her sweet spot easy to find...

So ends another exciting chapter...
As I escape this wonton nest...
For I hope to end my story...
Resting softly on an honest breast...

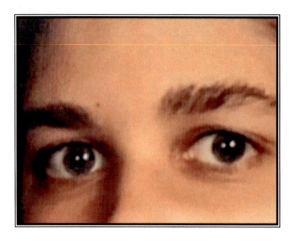

This Magical Moment

Her eyes sparkle like blue diamonds...
Her lips are rose bud red...
Her smile can bring me to my knees...
Thoughts of her always stay in my head...

I remember the day I met her...
Her manner was reserved and demure...
The more I tried to make eye contact...
The more she would glance towards the floor...

I think there was a slight moment...
That I witnessed her steal a quick glance...
Even if this thought was only in my mind...
I chose the opportunity to make my advance...

I moved quickly across the room...
To introduce myself as a new friend...
And never once, not even for a moment...
To be more than my initial intend...

But the more we spent time together...
And after the night of the Comus Ball...
All of a sudden, in a magical moment...
I felt myself beginning to fall...

It was into my arms she would cuddle...
As the stars sparkled bright in the skies...
It was at this magical moment...
I realized I had captured her eyes...

As our kisses became more full with passion...
That our togetherness began to show...
It was at this magical moment...
Our feelings began to grow...

As we celebrated our one week anniversary...
And we make future plans together as one...
It's as if this magical journey...
Was destined to have finally begun...

I feel blessed that you've entered my life...
And for joining me now and hereafter...
This magical journey we will embark together...
Full of excitement, love and laughter...

Stealing Slow Kisses

I love stealing slow kisses
And nibbling on your ear...
I love to gently pull you closer
So that we can be forever near...

I love to rub my fingers
Through your thick and curly hair...
I love to gaze into your eyes
As you hypnotize me with your stare...

I love when you press your body
Against mine, from head to toe...
Why it took so long to find you
The answer, I will never know...

But I'm glad we found each other
And for the joy you truly bring...
For it's a gift I will always cherish
From the mountaintop I will always sing...

Thank you for being in my life...❤️

I Love You True

I love our walks...
I love our talks...
I love our embrace...
I love your face...

I love our corner
Where we kiss at night...
I love the sound you make
When I hold you tight...

I love your curls...
I love your eyes...
I love the fact that
You love no other guys...

I love your lips
When they're kissing mine...
I love your taste
That is oh, so fine...

I love you, Jane...
And all you do...
I love you, Jane...
I love you true...

Our Corner

Sittin' on our corner...
Thinkin' about my girlfriend...
Missin' her sweet kisses...
Thinkin' she's my Godsend...

Cravin' her affection...
Needin' her attention…
Wantin' our sweet moments...
Trustin' our intention...

This Is What Defines Our Love

The chance to see the world anew through my lover's eyes;
This is what defines our love.

The grace to grow together by being each other's support;
This is what defines our love.

The reassurance that today will be good and right because a trustworthy friend is standing by me;
This is what defines our love.

The freedom to make mistakes and recover. To see that this is not falling or failure, but stepping stones;
This is what defines our love.

To know the truest sense of becoming alive and delighting in my lover's gift;
This is what defines our love.

Jane

August 12, 2020

You Don't Have To Say It

You don't have to say you love me
Because I see it in your eyes...
You don't have to say you miss me
Because I feel it in our long goodbyes...
You don't have to say I'm the only one
Because I can feel it in your embrace...
You don't have to say you love me
Because it shows in your beaming face...

Every day is a blessing
Because I have you in my life...
Every day is a gift from God
Because you take away all my strife...

Every time we are together
It's like a magical moment we have to share...
Every time we are apart
It's good knowing you soon will be there...

You don't have to say you love me
Because I see it in your eyes...
You don't have to say you miss me
Because I feel it in our long goodbyes...
You don't have to say I'm the only one
Because I can feel it in your embrace...
You don't have to say you love me
Because it shows in your beaming face...

The time we spend together
The new adventures that we create...
These experiences that we share
Are proof that you are my perfect mate...

Our future will be as exciting
As we both know it truly can be...
We are so blessed to have found each other
In our world of you and me...

You don't have to say you love me
Because I see it in your eyes...
You don't have to say you miss me
Because I feel it in our long goodbyes...
You don't have to say I'm the only one
Because I can feel it in your embrace...
You don't have to say you love me
Because it shows in your beaming face...

This is what defines us... ❤️

Holding On To Memories

Holding on to memories
Of jilted lovers last...
We must let go of their demons
Lurking from the past...

Until we lose the bastard's baggage
Living rent free in our mind...
Until we cleanse our angry thoughts
A new relationship we'll never find...

Holding on to memories
For jilted lovers lost...
We must let go of their demons
Put future happiness at a cost...

When sadness comes to visit me
It often has your face...
No matter how hard I try to find
Our happiness, there is no trace...

Holding on to memories
Until the morning dawn...
We must let go of our demons
Before our love for each other is gone...

If we can't find trust between each other
And our insecurities become the rule...
I'm no longer interested in seeing you
Because I refuse to play the fool...

The Amazing Turn

We met in a casual existence...
It was all very simple and kind...
She seemed to be a nice girl...
In my world, an impossible find...

It started as a real friendship...
We took our time and we talked...
We spent the next few weeks together...
Being open and honest as we walked...

It's started all so innocently...
On the afternoon of February 23rd...
It was raining softly against the window...
Neither of us spoke a single word...

It was nothing more than a friendship...
Until it took an amazing turn...
I was staring into her lovely eyes...
She kissed me slowly in return...

We held each other closely...
In a long and loving embrace...
I memorized each of her features...
As I stared affectionately at her face...

It was a moment I'll always remember...
The first and only time...
It's so hard to describe my feelings...
Unless to say it was totally sublime...

Our moments together became fulfilling...
The touching with more suspense...
The reliance more on each other...
Our moments together became more intense...

So there we were in a relationship...
That I thought might finally be real...
She seemed to the right one...
My heart, I allowed her to steal...

And then the moment happened...
Her eyes were filled with excite..
She said she wanted something different...
And she wanted it to last all night...

I'll admit I was very intrigued...
She wanted to reach a new height...
She told me to get under the covers...
She lit some candles; turned off the light...

As Marvin Gaye played in the distance...
She slipped quietly into my bed...
I asked her "what should I do?"
"Just relax..." and she massaged my head...

As she rubbed her fingers through my hair...
And leaned down to kiss my chest...
I tried to move my hands closer...
To gently fondle her panting breast...

She slowly pushed my hands away...
And whispered again into my ear...
"Tonight I just want you to relax, baby...
I'm going to say things I need you to hear..."

I tried to relax as she suggested...
But the intensity was hard to bare...
She continued to massage my throbbing head...
As she ran her fingers through my hair...

Then she slowly kissed my neck...
Nibbling affectionately on my ear...
She rubbed her hands along my back...
As she straddled across my rear...

She continued to rub my shoulders...
And licked me slowly down my spine...
I tried to turn over to embrace her...
She snapped "now stop that!"
Slapped me firmly and said "you're mine!"

At first I became a little shaken...
As she continued to rub my back...
Her firm and deep caressing...
Quickly put my train back on her track...

As she continued to stroke my backside...
And lick my skin with loving demure...
I fell unconsciously into her grasp...
Where only Psyche could find my cure...

She owned me body and mind...
It was as if she was combining our souls..
As she brought me deeper into her spell...
She quietly tied my hands to the bed poles...

Before I realized what had happened...
She had turned me over on my back...
My legs were also tied spread eagle...
This girl certainly had the knack!

She assured me "I want you to relax...
And let me bring you to a whole new place..."
She whispered "now, close your eyes..."
As she tied a silk cloth across my face...

I felt my body twitch and tingle...
As hot lotion landed here and there...

It seemed she had done this before...
Slim chance I was her first affair...

Nonetheless, I allowed her to control...
The situation, since I couldn't really move...
But be perfectly honest with you...
It seemed a situation I couldn't really improve...

As the night went on and on...
She did things I can't put into words...
I mean, she did things I certainly hadn't heard of...
When the coach taught us about the bees and the birds...

Then, once she was finally finished...
My entire body seemed spent and numb...
She cleaned me with a warm washcloth...
When she was finished she said "now, we're done!"

She cut the ropes with a saber...
Freeing me from her bed...
My clothes were near by, neatly folded...
My entire body tingling and red...

As I limped across the room...
It was a pain I actually enjoyed...
My first time to be totally dominated...
All captured by the Polaroid...

It was the last time I ever saw her...
She moved out the very next day...
My calls and emails went unanswered...
I guess that's how the dominatrix play...

I think of her now fairly often...
All the things we did that night...
I enjoyed being totally dominated...
Even when she drew blood from the backbite...

So if you ever get to meet her...
And she brings you to her room...
It will change your attitude forever...
One is certain to assume...

My Hundred Dollar Bill

It's hard to find the words
To explain the love I have for you...
It's hard to describe the bond we have
For me, there's nothing you wouldn't do...

This true everlasting friendship
Has never been some quid pro quo...
This unconditional brotherly love
Is all we've ever had to know...

Who needs a hundred singles
Or friendships we forever need to refill...
When I can always count on my best brother
My Hundred Dollar Bill...

We had so many experiences,
Mostly really good, but a few somewhat bad...
We've enjoyed so many times together
Some totally hilarious, but a few kinda sad...

We've learned from all our mistakes,
We've matured together, into good men indeed...
We've celebrated with much wine, women and song
But we never shared the evil weed...

Who needs a hundred singles
Or friendships we forever need to refill...
When I can always count on my best brother
My Hundred Dollar Bill...

When I started writing a poem
To describe my love I have for my brother...
It was in the middle of my rhymin'
I realized our friendship is the gift to one another...

I couldn't have ask Our Heavenly Father
For a kinder or better friend...
And I know you'll always be there for me
From then, to now and to the very end...

Who needs a hundred singles
Or friendships we forever need to refill...
When I can always count on my best brother
My Hundred Dollar Bill...

Best Friend Advice

Do you remember the time when that buddy...
Tried to give you their best friend advice...
They said "You don't really have to do this!"
And you didn't think they were being very nice...

You thought you had made the right decision...
You would be in love 'til death do you part'
You thought you had married the perfect girl...
Until on your wedding night, all she did was fart...

The next day she started spending your money...
A week later, she wrecked your favorite car...
Then she started demanding Big Os every night...
With that, she had now gone too far...

She was such a nice girl when you were dating...
During each one of those seven long years...
Now she's become a freakin nightmare...
No more nights out with the guys for some beers...

Before you even got settled...
She moved back to live with her mom...
Before long the divorce lawyer called you...
Your life is exploding like a bomb...

How in the world did all this happen...
You were living such a normal life...
Then all of a sudden everything is turned upside down...
That sweet girl became your new wife...

Your friends said 'We tried to warn you!'
'But no, you wouldn't listen to us!'
'Your whole life is now in a shambles...'
'You look like you've been hit by a bus!'

Sometimes it's best to listen to your buddies...
Especially when it comes to getting a wife...
You're true friends will always be there...
After she turns your entire world into strife...

He's My Piper Tim

As he stands up on the hill...
Wearing his kilt and a Zen-like grin...
I'm proud to call him my brother...
He's my family... he's my Piper Tim...

Whether he's playing Amazing Grace...
Or my favorite tune Danny Boy...
His gift of music brings to the world...
So much serenity... so much joy...

We share a spiritual awakening...
A gift from our High Power...
Just the presence in each other's lives...
Rewards us with our day's finest hour...

As he stands up on the hill...
Wearing his kilt and a Zen-like grin...
I'm proud to call him my brother...
He's my family... he's my Piper Tim...

Sometimes we sit and say nothing...
Looking out the window... sharing a smile...
For it's that gift of brother love we share...
Along with our slyness and beguile...

So I celebrate our true friendship...
And our mutual trust with this here verse...
I'm so lucky to have Tim in my life...
A real friendship of true universe...

As he stands up on the hill...
Wearing his kilt and a Zen-like grin...
I'm proud to call him my brother...
He's my family... he's my Piper Tim...

Chapter 2: Mardi Gras

My Mardi Gras Mary

When it's Carnival time
You can keep your vodka cranberry...
Dat's when I grab for my Mardi Gras Mary...

When da flambeau start dancin'
And da Bonez Men get all scary...
Dat's when I grab for my Mardi Gras Mary...

Party Gras all night till you wake the cemetery...
Dat's when I grab for my Mardi Gras Mary...

When da Zulu floats break down
And all da crowds start growin' wary...
Dat's when I grab for my Mardi Gras Mary...

When the rain clouds start gettin' dark
And the weather starts lookin' hairy
Dat's when I grab for my Mardi Gras Mary...

Party Gras all night till you wake the cemetery...
Dat's when I grab for my Mardi Gras Mary...

When I meet a pretty lady in da Quarters
But she says her name is Gary...
Dat's when I grab for my Mardi Gras Mary...

When she sees me wit my side girl
And I become da cat who swallowed da canary...
Dat's when I grab for my Mardi Gras Mary...

Party Gras all night till you wake the cemetery...
Dat's when I grab for my Mardi Gras Mary...

I Want To Fall In Love With A Mardi Gras Queen

I wanna fall in love
with a Mardi Gras queen...
Show her a side of New Orleans
that she's never seen...

Take her to the dark side
of the Marigny...
Show her my real world
without the bourgeoisie...

Take a streetcar ride
up the Avenue...
Take a horse and buggy ride
in the Quarters, too...

I wanna fall in love
with a Mardi Gras queen...
Introduce her to Veuve Clicquot
And my French cuisine...

Have a late night talk
on the Riverwalk...
Make a late night stop
at Jean Lafitte's Blacksmith Shop...

Take a late night stroll
over to Pirates Alley...
Take in a burlesque show
Introduce her to my Sally...

I wanna fall in love
with a Mardi Gras queen...
Show her a whole new world
at the couple's scene...

Rub my anxious fingers
through her long curly hair...
While slowly kissing her neck
near Jackson Square...

Take her home at night
and make her feel just right...
And then I'll rub her feet
Until she falls fast asleep...

I wanna fall in love
with a Mardi Gras queen...
Her daddy won't be happy
If you know what I mean...

A Mardi Gras Tree

I think that I
shall never see...
Anything as cool
as a Mardi Gras tree...

They grow in New Orleans
nearly every Spring...
As the bands start marching
in full swing...

The beads are flung
from near and far...
As the revelers stumble
from bar to bar...

The tourists take selfies
with the trees behind...
On every block
these trees they find...

The Mardi Gras tree
is such a beautiful sight...
As the party continues
late into the night...

So whenever you visit New Orleans
and you find a Mardi Gras tree...
Make sure you post a selfie
for all of us to see...

Will You Throw Me Dat Coconut

I've been waitin' in the rain for the Zulu Nation...
Standin' on the corner of Canal n' Basin...
I want to see dat king n' da marchin' tramps...
My arms are tired o' hangin' from da street lamps...

Da bands are jammin' and Mr. Big Shot be cool...
But I need a coconut or I'll feel like a fool...
So if I shake my Mardi Gras butt...
Will you throw me dat coconut...

I got all da beads I ever could need...
So stop trying to make me yell n' plead...
I don't need no damn Muse's shoe...
If I only catch one, den what's dat gonna do...

I love da floats and da Purple Knights...
Everyone is dancin' and dere ain't no fights...
It's so nice dat we all are gettin' along...
And I'm havin' fun just singin' dis song...

But what I really need to make me smile...
Is to catch a coconut every once in awhile...
So if I shake my Mardi Gras butt...
Will you throw me dat coconut...

The Krewe of Tucks is where I normally ride...
And dat's how I show my Mardi Gras pride...
If I try hard in life I could be anything...
But I hope one day to be da Mardi Gras king...

Now it's time to just wait my turn...
There are things in life I'll just have to earn...
Now if I shake my Mardi Gras butt...
Maybe I'll finally catch me dat coconut...

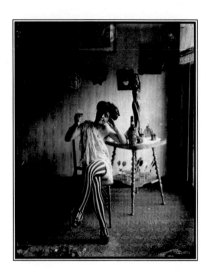

Mardi Gras Momma

Mardi Gras Momma
is so sweet and fine...
She works Bourbon Street
during Mardi Gas time...

Her hair is so long
and her booty is a shakin...
She wants a sugar daddy...
all his money she'll be a takin...

Mardi Gras Momma
won't you come home with me...
I'll be your Mardi Gras Daddy
and you can be my queen bee

She wants Mardi Gras beads
and she's willing to flirt...
She'll blow Mardi Gras kisses
and she'll pull up her shirt...

She'll dance da Mardi Gras mambo
and drink da hurricane...
She wants to wear a crown
and do the Mardi Gras reign...

Mardi Gras Momma
won't you come home with me...
I'll be your Mardi Gras Daddy
and you can be my queen bee...

She'll wear a fancy gown
and some high heel shoes...
She wants a sugar daddy
to see her private tattoos...

Will you take her home
to be your Mardi Gras queen...
She'll give you lots of babies
cuz she's only eighteen...

Mardi Gras Momma
won't you come home with me...
I'll be your Mardi Gras Daddy
and you can be my queen bee...

It's getting late at night
and da balls are almost done...
I think I'll take her home
and have some Mardi Gras fun...

When she wakes up in da morning
and has no idea where she is...
I'll pat her on the booty
and give her a glass of pop fizz...

Mardi Gras Momma
won't you come home with me...
I'll be your Mardi Gras Daddy
and you can be my queen bee...

Photograph: E. J. Bellocq

The Flambeau Nation

Here come the flambeau
on Mardi Gras night...
Bringing dark parades alive
by sharing their light...
When the sun goes down
and the nights get cool...
The Flambeau Nation
is the Mardi Gras rule...

They light parades at night
and scare aware the fright...
It's the Flambeau Nation
that makes Mardi Gras right...

It started way back then
In the time around 1875...
When the Flambeau Nation
first became alive...
The Mardi Gras floats
were pulled by a single mule...
And the flambeau lights
kept away the freakish ghoul...

The flambeau carriers
were a very special breed...
They had to be really strong
and they had to have speed...
Many were blood related,
brothers and cousins too were there...
That's why the flambeau tradition
remains a strong family affair...

They light parades at night
and scare aware the fright...
It's the Flambeau Nation
that makes Mardi Gras right...

Sometimes it gets really spooky
when no flambeau are around...
You go down the wrong street
and your heart starts to pound...
You hear footsteps around you,
the hair stands on your neck...
But here comes the flambeau light,
you're no longer a freakin wreck...

The flambeau have been a tradition
for a dozen or more decades...
Without the Flambeau Nation
we might not have night parades...
So throw out as many dollars
as tonight your wallet can spare...
Cuz without the Flambeau Nation,
night parades might not be there...

They light the parades at night
and scare aware the fright...
It's the Flambeau Nation
that makes Mardi Gras right!

Photograph: Skip Bolen

The Mardi Gras Indians

Right after the turn of the century
The Mardi Gras Indians came alive...
The tribes came from all over the city
From the different wards where they still survive...

Downtown Indians use sequins and feathers...
Uptowners use feathers, rhinestones and beads...
The main part of every costume is the patch...
A message from the heart is what it reads...

After a year of making their costumes
Using all the velvet and sequins galore...
The chiefs are ready to share their magic
And keep their costumes a secret no more...

Spy Boy stands out in front
Making sure no tribes are near...
He communicates with First Flag
In case a gang is sharing fear...

Once the Big Chief gets his signal
He leads the tribe safely through the hood...
He protects his tribe from danger
as any brave Mardi Gras Chief should...

When two tribes would come together
They use to settle any bad score...
But today the tribes are friendly
And gang fighting they do no more...

'Me no Humba', you be Humba'
Is what one Chief says to the other...
At the end of the Mardi Gras season
All the tribes become one, my brother...

Photograph: Ryan Hodgson-Rigsbee

The King Cake Baby

As January 6th approaches
A cautious excitement fills the air...
For all throughout New Orleans
Arrive the King Cakes with Mardi Gras flare...

As the King Cake boxes arrive
At schools and offices all around...
We cut the King Cakes and sink our teeth
Into a delicious sugary mound...

As purple, gold and green sugars
Sparkle majestically in the light...
The buttery cinnamon flavor
Makes our tastebuds dance in delight...

Then we all begin to wonder
As our mouths water and hope that maybe...
We might just be the lucky one
To receive the King Cake Baby...

For whoever receives the Baby
As the tradition has always been...
It's your turn to bring a new King Cake
Tomorrow morning when you come in...

So enjoy your Mardi Gras season
As the King doth often command...
Always love your King Cake Baby
And Happy Mardi Gras throughout the land!

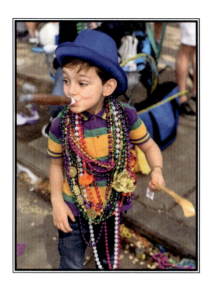

Here Come Da Parades

We got da ladders standing
And da side streets are all guarded.
We got da flambeaux fired up
Let's get dis Mardi Gras started.

Krewe du Vieux, Krewe of Cork,
And da mighty Krewe of Oshun.
Here come da Mardi Gas parades,
Let's start up da commotion!

Where Ya'at Cleopatra,
Where Ya'at Pontchartrain.
Let's catch some Mardi Gras beads
While we standin' in da rain!

Uptown's got Choctaw and Freret,
And da Marigny has 'tit Rex.
Dere's a party goin on
At your momma's stucco duplex.

Give me some Sparta, and Pygmalion
And some Krewe of Carrollton.
Here come all da parades,
Let's start havin' us some fun!

Here comes da Krewe of Alla
And da Krewe of King Arthur, too.
Here comes da Krewe of Barkus
With all dere doggy poo!

Here's da Ancient Druids
And da Mystic Krewe of Nyx.
If I wear my costume,
Will I meet some pretty chicks?

Here come da Knights of Chaos
And da Knights of Babylon.
The Mardi Gras parades have started So let's get this party on!

Here comes the Krewe of Muses
With all those silly girls.
I hope to catch a fancy shoe
From a lady in pink curls!

And dere's da Krewe of Hermes,
Next Le Krewe d'Etat,
Followed by Krewe of Morpheus.
Dis is how da Who Dats play!

Here's come da Krewe of Iris,
Followed by da Krewe of Tucks.
I want me a toilet plunger
And some plastic Mardi Gras cups!

Da chefs have dere Krewe of Lafcadio,
And da Yats have da Endymion ball.
Put on your gown, put up your hair,
Let's party down one and all!

Here comes da Krewe of Okeanos,
Den Mid-City and da Krewe of Thoth.
Next dere's da Krewe of Bacchus
We havin' fun now dawlin', you and me both!

But den dere's da Krewe of Orpheus,
Wit da bands and super floats.
They pull out all dere Mardi Gras best.
Da crowd is yellin' wit positive votes!

When I finally get up on Mardi Gras Day
I jump on my lil scooter and go out to play.
If I get downtown and shake my Mardi Gras butt
I hope to finally catch me a Zulu coconut!

And then I'll catch Rex
And da Crescent City trucks.
I wouldn't trade in my Mardi Gras day
For nothing short of a million bucks!

Happy Mardi Gras to your momma
And to da Wild Tchoupitoulas, too.
I love kissin' on dem PussyFooters!
How 'bout you!

Mardi Gras Chihuahua

My name is Boudreaux and I'm a Mardi Gras Chihuahua...
I live in Uptown New Orleans and I have friends all over the world...
They think that I am lucky to live in New Orleans...
Because the king cake is tasty and the Mardi Gras season seems to last forever...

My friends come to visit at the same time every year...
We like to wear costumes and dress up real crazy...
We look so cute and have our pictures taken by people...
We play so hard all day then at night we get very sleepy...

My little brother is Thibodaux and he loves to dress up, too...
He lives in the Marigny and he likes to dress up for his friends...
Sometime she looks silly in his sequins and pink tutu...
He often looks funny in his gold high-heeled shoes...

His friends love to visit and dance to Broadway show tunes...
Thibodaux and his buddies love to be in the parades...
Their costumes are so glitzy and sparkle in the flambeau lights...
They wear lots of boa feathers and even fishnet stockings...

But Thibodaux is my brother and I love him just the same...
Even when he tries to eat my food, he can be such a pain...
He loves Mardi Gras and to be with all his buddies...
Mardi Gras puts a smile on his face and a gleam in his eyes...

I have a sister named Lacey who lives in Mid City...
While I am a small Chihuahua, Lacey is really itty bitty...
She acts like a princess in her beautiful silk costume...
She always makes a grand entrance when arriving in any room...

She has dozens of Chihuahuas who lineup for her attention...
Lacey loves to be noticed and to be hugged by everyone...
She's always very happy and loves to be held...
Mardi Gras is the time of the year Lacey loves the most...

All the Mardi Gras Chihuahuas get together on Mardi Gras day...
We can't wait to wear our costumes and be in the Krewe of Barkus parade...
We walk along the parade route and all the people cheer...
The hand us doggy treats and tell us we look so cute...

Maybe this year I'll meet some new friends...
And we can become best friends only like Chi doggies can be...
All of us will have on beautiful costumes with colors so bright...
We'll have fun all Mardi Gras day and then go to sleep late at night...

Chapter 3:
New Orleans History

Marie Laveau: The Voodoo Queen

There once was a priestess
Born a long time ago...
A famous voodoo queen...
Named Marie Catherine Laveau...

She was born in the French Quarter
Back in 1801...
And within a matter of years
Her powerful work had begun...

She was born a wealthy creole
A person of color who was free...
Her father was a noble, gentle man
Her mother was pretty, part Cherokee...

Marie married in the St Louis Cathedral
To a man named Jacque Paris...
She quickly had a daughter
And then the newlyweds were three...

Jacque was a good carpenter
Building tables, chairs and more...
He truly loved his beautiful Marie
And soon there were four...

Shortly thereafter the last birth
Her beloved Jacque was to die...
That left young Marie and her babies
On their own journey to get by...

So she opened a beauty salon
Making house calls to the rich...
She learned all their secrets
Promising to never ever snitch...

But soon she discovered their secrets
Could be kept for a hefty price...
She would create secret potions
From ancient recipes with much spice...

She learned early on
To use her powers with refrain...
As her ability to cast spells
Should never be used in vain...

She practiced her voodoo
While employed as a midwife...
It was her ability to cast spells
That caused bad people much strife...

But then in June of 1881
Her life finally came to an end...
She was surround by her family
And Glapion, her lifelong boyfriend...

Marie Laveau and her history
Have been surrounded by legend and lore...
But as of that one fateful evening
Her voodoo would be practiced never more...

The rumor has Marie buried in a tomb
Located in St Louis #1 cemetery...
But we will truly never know
As Marie's spirit will remain legendary...

Hurricane Katrina: She Couldn't Wash Away New Orleans

Hurricane Katrina couldn't wash away our culture.
She couldn't wash away our spirit, couldn't wash away our pride.
She couldn't wash away our music or how we like to party.
She could never kill New Orleans, no matter how hard she tried.

She blew into New Orleans in late August, '05.
She smashed into our levees like a fast pitch line drive.
Thousands of our people weren't ready for her anger.
She'll go down in our history as a mean Category 5.

Soon our weak levees gave way to her meanness.
The brown water covered most of our beloved city.
While the rest of the country shook their heads in dismissal.
New Orleans' survival was indeed not looking pretty.

But the Who Dats stare danger right back in its face.
As a family we gather around and as a community we embrace.
The people of New Orleans don't take nothin' lying down.
We're the Who Dat Nation! We're the talk of the town!

Hurricane Katrina couldn't wash away our culture.
She couldn't wash away our spirit, couldn't wash away our pride.
She couldn't wash away our music or how we like to party.
She could never kill New Orleans, no matter how hard she tried.

Once the water left our City and our people came back home.
It was time to clean up our houses and our beloved Superdome.
Soon arrived the Neville's, The Dirty Dozen and Dr. John
Then came the Radiators and our jukebox was turned on.

Vince Vance & The Valiants returned and the Wild Magnolias too.
And Harry Connick arrived with his entire sound crew.
Then Deacon John, Irma Thomas and Allen Toussaint
'They All Axed for You' was playin' without no restraint!

Hurricane Katrina couldn't wash away our culture.
She couldn't wash away our spirit, couldn't wash away our pride.
She couldn't wash away our music or how we like to party.
She could never kill New Orleans, no matter how hard she tried.

When our own Fats Domino finally arrived back on the scene
People started to smile again cuz New Orleans was getting clean.
They started cooking gumbo and the Saints started to win.
New Orleans was finally back on its dancin' feet again.

Soon the snowball machines were humming
and the parades were running on schedule.
The king cakes were baking and we could buy Roman candy.
Shrimp were getting boiled and crawfish were getting peeled.
The people started smiling cuz the Katrina wounds were getting healed.

Hurricane Katrina couldn't wash away our culture.
She couldn't wash away our spirit, couldn't wash away our pride.
She couldn't wash away our music or how we like to party.
She could never kill New Orleans, no matter how hard she tried.

Whispering Spirits Among The Old Oak Trees

Nestled among the old oak trees...
Live the spirits who visit each day...
They usually appear early in the morning...
If you listen closely you can hear them say...

"You thought you may have buried us...
But our spirits won't bid you adieu...
You can never change who we truly are...
We're a part of your historical roux..."

Jean Lafitte, in all his splendor...
A pirate by day and night...
He helped win the Battle of New Orleans...
He led his pirates in a victorious fight...

There's the famous voodoo priestess...
Her name was Marie Laveau...
A voodoo queen of New Orleans...
Her legend will forever grow...

The great American General...
Whose name was Robert E. Lee...
He fought against Northern aggression...
To earn his place in Southern history...

Then there was Huey P. Long...
A shady politician who could never fail...
If an assassin hadn't ended his life...
He probably would have ended up in jail...

Homer Plessy was an activist...
Always fighting for his civil rights...
When he wasn't trying to get a seat on the train...
He would argue for the colored man's plights...

Louis Armstrong was the jazz trumpet master...
Around the world he would roam...
He honed his craft in Chicago...
But New Orleans he always called home...

Truman Capote was a squirrelly boy...
Who spent his summer on the coast...
While he could spin a wonderful tale...
His Breakfast At Tiffany's was more than dry toast...

Who could forget Lee Harvey Oswald...
Nothing more than a bumbling shrug...
Until he shot John F. Kennedy...
Becoming New Orleans' most infamous thug...

Then there was Miss Leah Chase...
She was a caring mother to us all...
Dishing creole food and expert advice...
To American presidents, both short and tall...

Nestled among the old oak trees...
Whispering spirits who visit each day...
They're always part of our story...
If you listen closely you can hear them say...

"You thought you may have buried us...
But our legends will forever increase...
You can never change who we truly are...
But from our history may you all learn peace..."

Image: Alexey Sergeev

They Call It Pirates Alley

There once was a dark, steamy alley
As the story has often been told...
That was frequented by frightful pirates
Often smelly, crusty and old...

Jean Lafitte and his many pirates
Used this alley to sell their wares...
They paid off the local police
To move their booty without any cares...

Since the adjacent building known as the Cabildo
Housed the local corrupt City Hall...
Where many a crooked politician
Would so often come to call...

The pirates and their politicians
Traded peacefully among one another...
Which offered a very nice living
For Jean, and also Pierre, his big brother...

The local jail was located in the alley
Where his partner, pirate Pierre...
Who was alway drunk and disorderly
Would often end up punished in there...

After breaking Pierre out
Of the old Spanish calaboose...
The Lafitte boys and their pirates
Would pack up and quickly vamoose...

It is said that a secret meeting
Was held between Lafitte and Andrew Jackson...
Where together they discussed a plan
To defeat the British for all their taxin'...

Lafitte would supply his pirates,
His artillery and swamp expertise...
All designed to help General Jackson's army
Bring the powerful British to their knees...

After the Battle of New Orleans was fought
And General Jackson's army had finally won...
Was when the General formally acknowledged
Jean Lafitte's pirates, and an Ursuline nun...

It was also said that William Faulkner
Rented a secluded flat there, in late 1925...
It's where his story 'Soldier's Pay'
Would eventually be written and come alive...

In 1830, it became a cobblestoned alley
As it is still to this very day...
It's also known as the alley
Where Morgus the Magnificent was known to play...

So in 1964, to finally make permanent
What had long been already claimed...
The famous street "Pirates Alley"
Became officially what is was named...

So whether you're walking on Pirates Alley
In the early morning or late at night...
If you see the ghost of a pirate
Say "Hello, Jean Lafitte" instead of running in fright...

The Majestic Oaks

As one walks quietly among the majestic oaks...
They could only imagine the stories these trees could tell...
From the romantic tales of unrequited love...
To the Southern gentleman consoling an unsuspecting young belle...

The stories about the first lovers...
Who embraced deeply in lust...
And loved each other as only teenagers do...
Long into the twilight of the evening dusk...

And the adoring married couple...
Spreading the picnic blanket under the shade...
The husband would read sweet poetry...
Sharing a lunch his young wife had dutifully made...

And then there were the children...
Running around playing hide and go seek...
They would run so hard from tree to tree...
Until they tired themselves into an afternoon sleep...

And while the stories one could have imagined...
Would often be all cheery and bright...
Other times the stories might tell a sad tale...
One of darkness and woeful plight...

Like the hanging of the young man...
Whose crime was stealing a horse...
As a teenager fighting for the rebels...
He was no match against the strong Union force...

Or the black man in search of his freedom...
To find his beloved family was all he could hope...
Silently walking North along the banks of Bayou St. John...
His young life finished at the end of a rope...

And the stories abound of the Dueling Oaks...
Where unimportant scores were settled to the death...
It's among these trees where lives were cut short...
Where many a fool took his last dying breath...

But today the stories are different...
As thousands come here to play...
The majestic oaks tell a different story...
One of friendship and finding a better way...

It is among the majestic oak trees...
That our thoughts are spoken as forgotten care...
So that we become one, together, with nature...
In what we refer to as a spiritual affair...

Image: The Dueling Oaks, City Park

Historic New Orleans Streetcars

The Historic New Orleans Streetcars
First drawn by horses in 1832...
Connected Lake Pontchartrain to the Mississippi River
Along beautiful Elysian Fields Avenue...

This was soon followed
By the Poydras-Magazine Line...
And then Lafayette (Jackson) and Nayades (St. Charles),
Totally by design...

Everyone loves the streetcar
When it's coming down the track...
If you want to see New Orleans by streetcar
You can take it there and back...

In the year 1850
Even more streetcar lines came about...
With the Louisiana and Napoleon Lines
The Uptown Rulers began to clap and shout...

The years of 1860 and 1861
Saw major expansion for our historic streetcars...
The Magazine, Camp and Dauphine Lines were added
Bringing even more citizen applause...

Everyone loves the streetcar
When it's coming down the track...
If you want to see New Orleans by streetcar
You can take it there and back...

The electric cars soon arrived
Clickety clacking along in 1893...
Eventually combining our people with commerce
For more than a century...

A Streetcar Named Desire
Was written by Tennessee Williams, in 1945...
It's considered a great American literary achievement
But not enough to keep the Desire Line alive...

Everyone loves the streetcar
When it's coming down the track...
If you want to see New Orleans by streetcar
You can take it there and back...

The St. Charles Avenue Streetcar
Is the one and only streetcar line...
To continuously operate in New Orleans'
Throughout our historic streetcar's time...

Most of the old streetcar lines
Are no longer in use today...
Replaced by cars and most recently bicycles
As our historic city gets lost in the fray...

Everyone loves the streetcar
When it's coming down the track...
If you want to see New Orleans by streetcar
You can take it there and back...

The good old glory days
Of the Historic New Orleans Streetcars...
Will eventually be faded from memory
As our way of life changes with progressive laws...

The wonderful days of old
When we could go round trip for a shiny nickel...
Will soon see our beloved streetcars
Retired like a plate with a half-eaten pickle...

Everyone loves the streetcar
When it's coming down the track...
If you want to see New Orleans by streetcar
You can take it there and back...

Image: Historic New Orleans Streetcars

Irma Thomas: Our Soul Queen

Irma Thomas, you're the soul queen of New Orleans...
Irma Thomas, starting back in your early teens...
You were making men swoon in the music canteens...
They all wanted Irma, by any and all means...

Irma Thomas, Irma Thomas, Irma Thomas, Irma Thomas

'You can have my husband, but don't mess with my man...'
Said Irma to the ladies like no other woman can...
Her voice is like an angel, and her skin like caramel...
From her lips comes nectar, making every man's heart swell...

Irma Thomas, Irma Thomas, Irma Thomas, Irma Thomas

You're the lady in my heart and I've got you in my sight...
If it's ever cold and raining, I'll be there to hold you tight...
If you want someone to care, I'll be the answer to your prayer...
I love you Irma Thomas and I'll always be there… for you...

Irma Thomas, Irma Thomas, Irma Thomas, Irma Thomas

Irma Thomas, you're the soul queen of New Orleans...
Irma Thomas, Irma Thomas, you're the star of all my dreams...
Your sweet voice is what I hear at night before I fall asleep...
It's listening to your voice, that into heaven I soon shall leap...

Irma Thomas, Irma Thomas, Irma Thomas, Irma Thomas

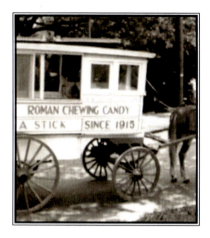 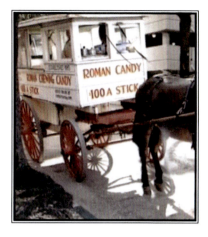

The Roman Candy Man

It all started back in 1915...
When a great grandmother named Angelina Napoli Cortese...
Made her candy for family and friends...
"The best in the world" is what everyone says...

Her son, Sam, was a 12 year old child...
A businessman at a very young age...
He started selling his momma's candy...
Working hard to make an honest wage...

Her candy was selling so fast
And Sam needed to meet the demand...
He soon employed a buggy and Aida...
Making the candy inside by hand...

Soon all the children were yelling...
"Momma, it's the Roman Candy man..."
Buying chocolate, vanilla and strawberry...
Sam was making it as fast as he can...

Selling for a nickel a stick until 1970...
It became everyone's treasured delight...
Even after more than a century...
It remains the dessert choice each and every night...

So when your kids start yelling for Roman Candy...
And the doggies begin to bark...
The vote is unanimous for Roman Candy...
Pull over in the front of Audubon Park...

Image: Historic Roman Chewing Candy

The Hyams Fountains

The Hyams Wading Fountains
For all New Orleans to enjoy...
Lovely gifts to all our children...
So much more than just a toy...

To us from Sara Lavinia Hyams...
A lovely lady of great wealth....
She sold her jewels and her riches...
To spread happiness and good health...

One fountain for each park...
Was her gift from Up Above...
These fountains were graciously given...
To our children with so much love...

Fountains of friendship...
For our children, old and young...
Gifts to all New Orleans...
For us to enjoy the Summer fun...

So splash away little children...
Throw caution to the wind...
As it was her wish for us all...
To enjoy her fountains 'til the end...

Chapter 4:
Humor and Limericks

Me Days Of Drinkin'

I miss me days of drinkin'
And all the joys of a wonderful life...
I ruined it all with a marriage
To an unforgivin' and bitter wife...

I enjoyed me pints of Guinness
Often chasin' them wit a dram of whiskey...
The more I drank, the braver I became,
Gettin better lookin' and sometimes even frisky...

Then late one cool fall evenin'
I tried to sneak a wee sloppy kiss...
When all of a sudden I was layin' flat on me back
Not realizin' she was another man's miss...

I jumped to me feet and shouted
"Do you have any idea who I am?"
This broad shouldered fellow just looked over to me and shouted
"I don't really give a damn!"

"You come in here every night
And you drink yourself into a stupor...
And then you start actin like Peter O'Toole
Until I knock you flat on your pooper!"

"It was all just a big misunderstandin,"
I tried to explain to this large young man...
He replied, "If you mess with me girl one more time
I'll put my boot in your scrawny little can!"

I suddenly had an epiphany
that me drinkin' was gettin' a bit much...
As I desperately tried to free me throat
away from this man's tightenin' clutch...

As the other men pulled this guy off me
And stopped him from splittin' me head...
It suddenly dawned on me drunkin' self
That is was past time for me to go to bed...

As I quietly slipped through me back door
And tiptoed slowly into me bed...
I suddenly felt a cold wet mop
Hit squarely across the back of me head...

It was at that moment I realized
I had better explain to the wife...
"That because I was defendin' ye honor
That I had barely escaped with me life..."

She quickly said she was sorry
And pushed me achin' head against her soft breast...
As I settled peacefully into me lady's arms
And finally got a good night's rest...

I have since sworn off the Guinness
And put me bottles of whiskey away...
I know longer fancy other men's ladies
As me own wife becomes more tolerable each day...

I really don't miss me drinkin'
Or comin' home to get smacked by me wife...
For today me marriage is blissful
With all the joys of a wonderful life...

Image: Peter O'Toole – Hellraiser, Sexual Outlaw, Irish Rebel, by Darwin Porter and Danforth Prince

My Cup o' Jane

When I'm waiting for the streetcar
And all of a sudden it begins to rain...
I start praying for some sunshine
And my little Cup o' Jane...

Cup o' Jane
Cup o' Jane
Oh, will she be my Cup o' Jane?

When I'm sitting on the runway
And they won't let us deplane...
I start hoping for a gate change
And my little Cup o' Jane...

Cup o' Jane
Cup o' Jane
Oh, will she be my Cup o' Jane?

When I'm working at the gym
And my back starts feelin' the pain...
I start wishing for a rub down
And my little Cup o' Jane...

Cup o' Jane
Cup o' Jane
Oh, will she be my Cup o' Jane?

When I'm jogging up Chestnut Street
And a pothole gives me an ankle sprain...
I start begging for some crutches
And my little Cup o' Jane...

Cup o' Jane
Cup o' Jane
Oh, will she be my Cup o' Jane?

When we finally start to celebrate
And suddenly realize there's no Champagne...
I know that life is so much sweeter
With my little Cup o' Jane...

Cup o' Jane
Cup o' Jane
She'll always be my Cup o' Jane!

Vesparado

Vesparado, will you take me for a ride...
I'm young and I'm pretty...
We can ride together, side by side...

If you let me ride with you
I'll treat your Vespa real fine...
You must be so lonely
Riding by yourself all the time...

I'm just kinda curious
About all the thoughts in your head...
There's no reason to be alone
We can ride together instead...

When we're riding and it starts raining
We can snuggle under an old cypress tree...
We'll stay warm and dry together
You, your Vespa and little ole me...

When the sun goes down
And the stars twinkle bright...
I'll keep you and your Vespa
Warm and snuggly all night...

And then early, tomorrow morning,
When the birds sing and the squirrels play...
We can ride off together on your Vespa
As we start a new and exciting day...

Image: Anita Ekberg, as Sylvia, La Dolce Vita – Directed by Federico Fellini

A Snowball From Sal's

When my chips are down
And I'm feeling blue...
My car has a flat
And da rent is past due...

My wife just left me
And she took my dog...
My thoughts are all confused
Cuz my head's in a fog...

While I won't be lonely
Cuz I know plenty of gals...
But all I really need
Is a snowball from Sal's...

A snowball from Sal's...
A snowball from Sal's...
All I really need
Is a snowball from Sal's...

When da fish aren't bitin'
But da mosquitoes are...
I forgot to pay my tickets
and dey just towed my car...

My kids don't call me
Unless dey want money...
I enjoy writin' poems
But no one really thinks dere funny...

While I won't be alone
Cuz I got plenty of pals...
But all I really need
Is a snowball from Sal's...

A snowball from Sal's...
A snowball from Sal's...
All I really need
Is a snowball from Sal's...

Alligator Transportation

Alligator transportation...
Go in style crocodile...
In da swamps of New Orleans...
Or on da river called da Nile...

When your gettin's stopped a goin'...
When you're late for your date...
When your bees stopped a buzzin'...
She's sick and tired you're always late...

When your car stops a startin'...
And da bus never shows...
When your feet stop a runnin'...
Cuz you stubbed all your toes...

Alligator transportation...
Go in style crocodile...
In da swamps of New Orleans...
Or on da river called da Nile...

When your girl starts a naggin'...
Cuz she been waitin' all night...
But you can't seem to get there...
Nothin' seems to be goin' right...

At last you finally get dere...
Gettin' dere as fast as you can...
Only to find dat your naggin' girlfriend...
Decided to leave you for another man...

Alligator transportation...
Go in style crocodile...
In da swamps of New Orleans...
Or on da river called the Nile...

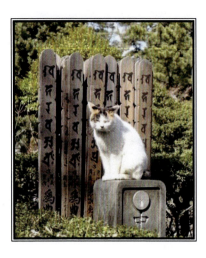

The Cemetery Pussycat

Pussycat, pussycat, where have you been?
I've been to the cemetery to visit my late master...
Pussycat, pussycat, what did you do there?
I tried to awake her by scratching the plaster...

Pussycat, pussycat, did she wake up from her sleep?
I was unable to wake her so I rested near her feet...
Pussycat, pussycat, what then did you do?
I chased away a mouse who was nibbling on her shoe...

Pussycat, pussycat, will you go back there again?
Yes, and if I see that mouse I'll mix him in my chow mein…
Pussycat, pussycat, why are you so gory?
Because now I am hungry and that's the end of this story...

Poetry From The Soul

We make music for our loved ones...
It's like poetry from the soul...
There's no need to make a request...
For it's your heart I wish to console...

Whether you like it jazz or blue...
No matter what the sound...
The goal is to have a tranquil effect...
To calm your anxiety down...

When your world is all a flutter...
And your thoughts are all confused...
It's through the gift of music...
The angst you'll begin to lose...

So allow yourself some solace...
And regain your peace of mind...
For it's through this gift, if you accept...
Peace and love you soon will find...

Image: Slim Aarons

Playing My Magic Horn

Since I was a young boy
I played my magic horn...
If my memory serves me
I played the first day I was born...

Instead of crying for momma's milk
All I wanted was to play Dixieland...
Instead of going off to play dates
I wanted to travel with my band...

While the other kids ignored me
They thought I was crazy in the head...
But instead of playing with dolls or guns
I wanted to play and earn some bread...

Not everyone finds their calling
Or their special purpose in life...
But I'm just happy making magic
Avoiding other people's strife...

So it's with my magic horn
That I will play forever more...
And if you don't like my music
Then walk yourself right out the door...

Photograph by Michael P. Smith

All Betts Are Off

They sat there on the comfortable sofa...
In the quiet of her living room...
That soon they would be embracing
Together as one he was to assume...

But that moment never materialized...
As he shot glances directed her way...
She was fully entranced with the telly
It became clear it wasn't his day...

It was impossible to read the situation...
He was no longer in control...
The outcome had become unpredictable...
She was resistant to his clever cajole...

His irresistible charm was failing...
His come hither lines were rebuked...
No matter how Latin his accent became...
It was apparent she couldn't be duped...

So when he suggested they kiss
She finally began to scoff...
He arrived at the inevitable conclusion
That all chances with Betts were off...

So he acted the proper gentleman
As he quietly licked his wounds...
And watched the rest of the movie
In kinship with broken hearted buffoons...

As soon as the movie was over
The thought of dessert was nowhere in sight...
He made haste to exit the opened door
And rode off into the cold, lonely night...

Sometimes we might have to step backwards
To move forward in one's game...
For to capture a lady's affection
One must move slowly to light her flame...

But as all interested women will tell you
That even though he struck out tonight...
While he may have lost this one battle
One must never give up the fight...

Be A Good Friend

Friends are important...
They are like gifts from above...
And befitting Josie and Chloe...
Like a hand and a glove...

Sometimes they share their secrets...
Other times they share their jokes...
Sometimes they act mischievous...
When planning a girlish hoax...

Sometimes they enjoy picnics...
On a bright sunny day...
They share their thoughts together
In a kind and caring way...

Sometimes friends like to giggle...
And roll around on the rug...
Friends are always there for one another...
With a kind word or just a hug...

So the next time when your sidekick...
Reaches out when they're in need...
Always be there for your girlfriend...
And be a good friend, indeed...

My New Home On Chestnut Street

My name is Roscoe...
This is my very own poem...
I recently moved to Chestnut Street...
To my very own new home...

I belong to Josie and Henry...
They've moved here with me, too...
We're excited about our new home...
It has two patios, who the heck knew...

I will miss all the familiar smells...
In my old hood where I walked each day...
But I look forward to my new adventures...
The chance of a new canine bouquet...

Maybe I'll make new friends...
With all the doggies on the block...
Maybe we'll have lots of play dates...
And chase cats round the clock...

Maybe we'll find lots of new bones...
Digging big holes of the neighbor's bed...
Maybe we'll bury old shoes...
Underneath the neighbor's shed...

I can't wait to walk along Chestnut Street...
With all the new adventures waiting for me...
It's going to be the best neighborhood in the world...
I'll leave my scent on every tree…

Our Moms: A Gift From Heaven

Birds of a feather
Flock together...
There's no stronger bond
Than a mom's love for her children...

Thank you, mom
For all you have done..
For me and our family
You were the one...

Who kept us together
Through thick and thin...
For carrying us all on your back
When we could no longer swim...

For being there
To clean our feathers...
For helping us dress
And buttoning our sweaters...

Thank you, mom
For teaching us about love...
You are truly a gift
From the heavens above...

The Technology Is Killing Us

IDK why I can't talk to my daughter...
I feel AWOL from her teenage life...
Our relationship has become all about texting...
I'm having the same problem with my wife...

So I was looking at my daughter's 📱...
To understand what's going on in her head...
But all I could find was gibberish...
In a text, this is all it said...

BF: OMG, you're a PYT...
Daughter: IDK, I have ADD, so just KISS...
BF: IRL, you're so PHAT...
Daughter: LOL, that's a BEG...
BF: BTW, I ❤ U in OT...
Daughter: OK, TTYL, but NTS...

I don't want to be a nosy father...
As I pride myself for being a 😎 dad...
But this lack of personal communications...
Is making me rather sad...

I miss the hugs and kisses...
From my children, and especially my wife...

Instead of real, deep discussions,
I get nothing more than 📱strife...

Wife: Can you make BLTs and do it ASAP! I'll be LFD tonight. BBL! 😘
Me: But when will you be home? I can't cook 🥓! It'll turn out FUBAR!
Wife: 😂 IDK, BBIAB, TTYL...✌️📱
Me: But I'm hungry! 🥺
Wife: LOL! OMG, you're so DOA! Just DIY... BRB! 👍📱😊

So I'm home by myself for dinner...
And I'm stuck here all alone...
My stomach is growling from hunger...
And I got nothing but this old 📱...

We use to be a very close family...
Having conversations at dinner, as we should...
But all this technology is killing us...
Simpler times are gone, in all likelihood...

Too Many Questions

How much time does it take
for water to stand still...
How long does it take
for a boy to get his thrill...

How much water does it take
for time to stop rushing...
How much confidence does it take
for a girl to stop blushing...

How much air does it take
for a bird to take flight...
How many fingers do you need
to count the stars at night...

How many hands does it take
for the gambler to get his flush...
How many questions does a child ask
before a parent says to hush...

What if a parent couldn't answer
all the questions a child could ask...
Should the child be forced to suffer
for putting the parent to such a task...

Chapter 5: Society and Politics

My Dad Was My Hero

My dad was a police officer...
He took a vow to faithfully serve...
He protected our friends and neighbors...
A man of courage and strong nerve...

He left for work one morning...
As he did most everyday...
He said "Mind your mother..."
It was just his normal way...

But at school that early morning...
The principal's aide came into my class...
My teacher called my name out loud...
And handed me a hall pass...

She couldn't look right at me...
But I noticed tears fell from her eyes...
Her face was red and her hands were shaking...
She seemed somewhat traumatized...

She told me to follow the aide...
That someone had come to call...
She said my momma needed me...
She said "Now, I want you to stand tall..."

I didn't quite understand...
What she was saying at that time...
Nothing seemed too real that moment...
My thoughts were all sublime...

As I entered the principal's office...
I saw my mom standing with our priest...
The last time I saw that look on their faces...
Was when my grandfather was deceased...

I said "Hello there mother!"
"Whatcha doing at my school?"
She took my little hands in hers...
And led me to the vestibule...

She said "Your dad was hurt at work today."
I immediately asked "Will he be alright?"
She looked me straight in the eyes...
And then she held my hands real tight...

"Your daddy was killed in action...
And he loved you very much...
Your daddy was very proud of you...
He wants you to be strong, as such..."

At first I was a bit confused...
And then I got really sad...
And then I can't remember what happened next...
As I was screaming for my dad...

My daddy was my hero...
He went off to protect our home...
I had no idea that morning...
He was going to leave us all alone...

I miss my dad more than ever...
The little things, like throwing a ball...
It's these times when everyone reminds me...
That my dad would want me to stand tall...

But people don't really understand...
They say things to try to be nice...
When you sign up to be a police officer...
It's your family that pays the price...

My daddy was my hero...
I am proud his uniform was blue...
I'll never forget you dad...
I'll never stop loving you...

Image: Aaron Thompson

The City That Care Forgot

With no one listening, who will hear the beautiful music on the streets of New Orleans...

With no one visiting, who will tip the bartenders and the waiters and the strippers...

With no one policing, who will stop the vandalism and the crime and the murder...

With no one governing, who will remove the dead bodies at the Hard Rock and finally give some peace and closure to the poor families who lost their loved ones...

With no one caring, who will be left to pick up the pieces of our once exciting and thriving city...

With no one loving, who will take care of our grandmothers who have done absolutely nothing to deserve these final years of decay and destruction of the very soul of New Orleans...

Photograph by David Dunn

Where Will The Old People Go?

Where will the old people go...
When the levees break...
And the water comes rushing in...

Where will the old people go...
When the water starts to rise...
And the politicians save only themselves...

Where will the old people go...
When our children are on crack...
And the opioid epidemic kills our grand babies...

Where will the old people go...
When our teenagers are dead in the streets...
And there's no one else to care...

Where will the old people go...
When the very people we elected fail to protect us...
And our grandmothers become vulnerable...

Where will the old people go...
When they can no longer fend for themselves...
And no one can hear them crying...

Where will the old people go...
When their world comes to an end...
And the only answer they receive is from Heaven...

Photograph: Alan Chin

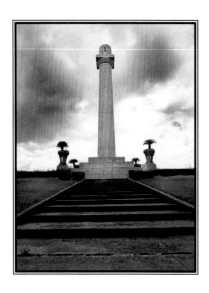

There Was A Time

There was a time...
When monuments were raised to great leaders...
Men and women of strong character...
People of great intellect and purpose...
Generals and scholars...
Spiritual and charitable...

A once beautiful and healthy city...
Vibrating with glorious festivals...
Of life, culture and community...
Families dancing with other families...
People of all walks of life...
celebrating as one, loving people...

There was a time...
When the simple minded people...
Elected bottom feeder politicians...
Men and women of weak moral fiber...
Raised on generations of fear and hate...
Carpetbaggers, pimps and community activists...
Godless, soulless and thieves...

Now the monuments say nothing...
As the soul is sucked out of the spirit...
Hollow screams from abandoned babies left to the care of tired grandmothers...
In a lost and deserted city...

There was a time...
When the past was removed and a future lost...
Destroyed in the name of cultural sensitivity...
The new normal...
Soon to be abandoned by the very politicians and community activists who stole our soul...

Photograph by Jay Rusovich

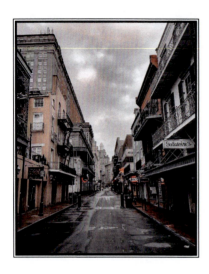

The Death Of New Orleans

Where have all the tourists gone...
Our politicians said to run along...

The coronavirus will kill us all...
But can we make one last pub crawl...

You'll get arrested if you do...
It's for our own safety, yes, me and you...

But who will pay the bouncers and whores...
If you lock up all the nightclub doors...

They'll receive a check from Uncle Sam...
That'll be enough for Ramen and Spam...

But who the hell will pay the rent...
Once the stimulus money has all been spent...

Then we'll go on welfare, yes, you and I...
And all the tourists will go bye-bye...

Photograph by Adrienne Ramos

Turn Out The Lights

The houses are dark...
The sky is grey...
Here in New Orleans
Life has gone away...

The schools are shut...
The kids don't play...
Where is everyone...
Why didn't anyone stay...

The music is gone...
And so is the food...
No one wants to play chess
So where the hell is Jude...

The office buildings are closed...
No one is at work...
City Hall is so corrupt
And the mayor is a jerk...

The streets are quiet...
The tourists are no more...
Someone turned out the lights
And locked the door...

Photo by David Dunn

The Politicians Don't Really Care

The cracked streets are quiet
and the clouds are all dark...
The French Quarter is eerily empty
as the criminals leave their mark...

The broken shutters are closed
and the iron gates are all locked...
The locals are too scared to come out
and the tourists are all shell shocked...

The drains can no longer handle
the rains from up above...
City Hall is a dismal failure
showing overtaxed locals no love...

The police are overwhelmed
and the politicians don't really care...
They expect the cops to succeed
on a wing and a frickin' prayer...

The jazz music is already gone
and the great chefs have all left town...
The pimps and their girls suffer
cuz there's no more money around...

What's happened to New Orleans
over the last few years...
Our children have all left us
Leaving the grandparents in tears...

We elected corrupt politicians
And they stole our very soul...
They left the heart of New Orleans
With nothing more than a flooded pothole...

Photograph: David Dunn

AssLetes

We used to praise you as our heroes
On the fields and on the courts...
We cheered you on so feverishly
In the world of professional sports...

We were proud to wear your jerseys
And memorized all your stats...
We were fiercely proud of you
We even called ourselves the Who Dats...

And then one day you decided
To dishonor our American Flag...
You knelt during our American Anthem...
Discarded us like a doggy poo bag...

So now when Benson's teams
Kneel to lace up your cleats...
We will forever refer to you
As nothing more than AssLetes...

You are no longer our heroes...
You are no longer athletes...
You ruined it all with your politics...
You are nothing more than AssLetes...

A Voodoo Curse For A Politician

Latoya Cantrell
You feckless fool...
This is a voodoo spell
To make you drool...

The voodoo priestess
Of New Orleans...
Will remove your wickedness
By any means...

The Who Dats have spoken
"She's an evil one!"
The spirits will haunt you...
There's no place to run...

Your skin will crawl
Right off the bone...
Your lying lips
Together will be sewn...

The blackened candle
Will burn your eyes...
You'll bleed from your ears
As New Orleans cries...

You're cursed Latoya
For your horrible deeds...
And for trying to remove
Our Mardi Gras beads...

Those parking tickets
Will slice your skin...
And peace you will know
Never ever again...

Your dark objectives
Will never be achieved...
Your horrific lies
Will never be believed...

The Hard Rock spirits
Will haunt you down...
They'll never stop
Until you leave town...

So leave New Orleans...
Never return again...
You're an evil woman...
May you live in shame...

What Is It That I See?

As I look across America
What is it that I see?
A once strong and proud republic
That was all about opportunity...

As I look across the land
What is it that I see?
Hungry little children
With their arms stretched out to me...

As I look across the sky
What is it that I see?
Flocks and flocks of lost birds
Seeking to land in a long lost tree...

As I look across the ocean
What is it that I see?
Angry people fighting one another
As their aging parents attempt to flee...

As I look across the heavens
What is it that I see?
Angels looking down sadly
As we no longer live peacefully...

Image: The statue of David is a masterpiece of Renaissance sculpture created in marble between 1501 and 1504 by the Italian artist Michelangelo.

Why Can't We All Just Get Along?

I know you're hurting because I feel your pain...
I hear it in your voice; your struggle is real...
I want you to know that I love and respect you...
It's time to forgive and find a new way to feel...

We need to communicate in a mutual dialogue...
Your rhetoric is filled with so much anger and fright...
Your pendulum swings so far to the left...
As I struggle so hard to treat you right...

We need to find our mutual peace and love...
For together we can be strong...
We only have one world to share...
Why can't we all just get along...

I keep trying to talk with you and keep you awake...
You tell me I'm wrong and you just want to stay woke...
But we have to keep working towards loving one another...
Before we both become emotionally broke...

Financial reparations aren't going to help find happiness...
Giving away something for nothing hasn't worked in the past...
We need to start working together to build our future...
We need to start loving each other or our world will never last...

We need to find our mutual peace and love...
For together we can be strong...
We only have one world to share...
Why can't we all just get along...

We need to find our mutual peace and love...
For together we can be strong...
We only have one world to share...
Why can't we all just get along...

We need to find our mutual peace and love...
For together we can be strong...
We only have one world to share...
Why can't we all just get along...

All Americans Matter!

I only kneel for God...
And I always stand for the American flag...
Let's be proud and stand together...
Let's stand tall and openly brag!

Black American lives matter...
White American lives matter, too!
Native American lives matter...
We're all together, me and you!

Now shout "All Americans Matter!"

Mexican American lives matter!
Canadian American lives, for sure!
We love all our visiting tourists...
But our borders must stay secure!

European American lives matter...
Asian American lives matter, too!
Gay and Straight lives matter...
Together, me and you!

Now shout "All Americans Matter!"

Jewish American lives matter...
Arab and Hindu Americans, too...
If we left someone out...
Hire a lawyer and try to sue!

We all need to get along...
That's what our forefathers had in mind...
We are Americans, first and foremost...
We are equal, as the Bill of Rights has defined...

So let's stop all this fighting...
Let's put our differences on the shelves...
We are all equal in the eyes of God...
And find some love among ourselves...

Now shout "All Americans Matter!"

Chapter 6: The Dark Side

Why Don't They Hear Me?

Why don't they understand me...
Why don't they hear me when I yell...
All these prescriptions are causing me problems...
I'm living my life in psychiatrist hell...

He never listens when I say I'm tired
Of all the crap they teach at school...
All he does is overdose me...
Face down on my desk in a puddle of drool...

My parents don't want me around...
They'll pay any amount to keep me away...
Why don't they hear me when I yell...
"The meds lead my feelings astray!"

He keeps trying to adjust my dosage...
I simply need my thoughts to cohere...
At what point will this shrink finally get it right...
He's been adjusting for over a year...

I beg my parents to understand me...
This pill pusher is driving me insane...
Why don't they hear me when I yell...
"It's the opioids that are causing my pain!"

Image: Actress Victoria Pedretti, starring in The Haunting of Hill House.

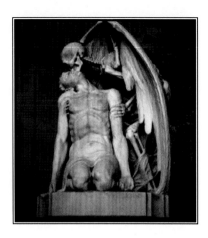

The Devil's Advocate

When you play the devil's advocate...
You're on the side of Satan...
When you venture to the dark side...
For your redemption, you'll be awaitin'...

If you go knockin' on Satan's door...
Sooner or later she'll invite you in...
She'll take you by the hand...
And seduce you with her grin...

Cuz once you're dancin' with the devil...
She'll want to keep you there all night...
And once you're in the devil's den...
You'll try to escape with all your might...

Once you're dealin' with the devil
She'll own your soul or she won't...
Better the angel that you know...
Than the devil that you don't...

So if you choosin' between good and evil...
Whether you go with naughty or nice...
Don't always go with your first choice...
Just take this old sinner's advice...

Image: "Kiss of Death" Barcelona

Her Stolen Innocence

When momma brought me home
I was hungry and I cried...
There was no one there to hug me
I was scared and I would hide...

When I accidentally soiled myself
I was whipped for being bad...
There was no one there to teach me
It was a childhood I never had...

When it was time to go to school
I was teased for being poor...
The other kids would call me names
They said my mother was just a whore...

When her man friends came to visit
They would look me up and down...
My momma would often yell at me
And say she didn't want me around...

When I would go outside alone
I often walked into the park...
I had to stay there playing by myself
Not going home till after dark...

When older boys would see me coming
They would call me over for a talk...
After they took turns hurting me
I was lucky to barely walk...

When I finally made it home
My momma told me I was no good...
She said I wouldn't be loved by anyone
Unless I left that neighborhood...

I ran away when I was thirteen
My momma's love I no longer yearned...
I chose the street life early on
My stolen innocence never to returned...

Even though I felt no hatred
For the momma I never really had...
I ended up living just like her
Unworthy, unloved and sad...

Photograph: Philip Jones Griffiths

Unrequited Love Gone Too Far

Valentine, Valentine,
Why do you refuse to be mine...
I send you expensive gifts
of red roses and fine wine...

I invite you to fancy restaurants,
And theatre and to the play...
You treat me with distain
And you tell me to 'stay away'

I said 'hi my sweetness'
When I saw you today at work...
You looked back at me and yelled
'Stop being such a damn jerk!'

Valentine, Valentine,
Why do you refuse to be mine...
I call you on your phone
And text you all of the time...

When I peer in your windows
And watch you in bed while you read...
It is all for you, my sweet love,
that I am truly in dire need...

I follow you all around town
When you're driving in your car...
I'd like to steal you away
And take you someplace really far...

Valentine, Valentine,
Why do you refuse to be mine...
I want to pack you in my suitcase
Tied up with my mother's red twine...

I dream of you every night
When I'm finally able to fall asleep...
But then I awake when you start screaming
'Leave me alone, you crazy creep!'

I tried to kiss you today
As you ran quickly down the street...
But then the police got between us
As they cuffed my hands and feet...

Now I have nothing but time
To think of us together again...
While I'm chained to my hospital bed
In this state hospital looney bin...

I See Things And I Wonder Why

I see precocious girls
with sadness on their faces...
Looking for daddy love
in all the wrong places...

I see craving little children
with hunger in their eyes...
Wondering why their mommas
are no longer in their lives...

Why does life have to be so hard
for the innocent and the young...
Why should they have to suffer
while their battles go unsung...

I see angry teenage boys
calling for the hero in their heart...
They simply want their dads in their lives
Where a jail cell won't keep them apart...

I see a grieving mother
who prays for her junkie daughter...
She prays the rosary for redemption
and bathes her daily in holy water...

Why does life have to be so hard
for the innocent and the young...
Why should they have to suffer
while their battles go unsung...

I see a lonely world of broken promises
filled with unfounded love...
I see so many praying for answers
but hearing nothing from up above...

Even though I try to see happiness
I only see unexplained pain and sorrow...
But if I keep on opening my eyes
will I finally see blessings tomorrow...

Why does life have to be so hard
for the innocent and the young...
Why should they have to suffer
while their battles go unsung...

Our lives will never be perfect
living in a world full of conflict and pain...
But why do the children have to live a life
filled with such hardship and daily strain...

Who Will Watch The Children?

Who will watch the children...
When the 32-year old grandmother is turning tricks to support her habit and her pimp is cashing her government checks...

Who will watch the children...
When there's no man in the house called daddy and the daughters are being turned over to the boyfriends when they reach the age of ten...

Who will watch the children...
When there's no food in the house and the now twelve year old momma/child has to feed the baby some solids...

Who will watch the children...
When the social worker and the community activists are fighting over what's best for the momma/child and her baby...

Who will watch the children...
When the now 15-year old momma/child is strung out and sold out by her momma's pimp, now called daddy by three generations of grief, despair and yet another failed government welfare program...

Who will watch the children...
When the hands of death are grabbing at the ankles of our future and there's no one there to save them...

Image: Staglieno Cemetery, Genoa - Italy, Italino Iacomelli Tomb, 1925, Sculptor: Adolph Lucarini

Ready To Strike...

Hello there, young lady...
I'm the voice of reason...
Now listen to me closely...
You're entering an exciting new season...

What your fickle parents taught you...
Wasn't all together real...
So I'm going to tell you something...
That will change the way you feel...

The world is your playground...
You can have anything you'd like...
Whatever you want, my love...
Your match is ready to strike...

My clever words of wisdom...
Will soon shed some new light...
It's time to leave your parents' world...
Now you're ready to take flight...

If you trust my words completely...
I think that you'll soon find...
I'm going to tell you something...
That's going to blow your mind...

The world is your playground...
You can have anything you like...
Whatever you want, my love...
Your match is ready to strike...

So come join me for this ride...
Throw caution to the wind...
Let me put your mind at ease...
I'm going to be your best friend...

If your offer me your mind...
I'll take your soul, as well...
And before you realize it, my darling
Your place will be with me in hell...

The world is your playground...
You can have anything you like...
Whatever you want, my love...
Your match is ready to strike...

You'll be my trusted confidant
Among my many friends below...
You'll be my brightest amber...
Your name they all will know...

So listen to me closely...
Take my hand, don't be afraid...
Let's take the journey down...
You'll be the trophy for my hand played...

The world is your playground...
You can have anything you like...
Whatever you want, my love...
Your match is ready to strike...

Image: Tomasz Alen Kopera

So Long World

As she stood in contemplation...
The thoughts of ending it were abound...
She could immediately stop the wretched suffering...
Her anguished soul never to be found...

All the agony; all the pain...
That lived each moment in her head...
Would finally leave forever more...
No more tears would she have to shed...

Why was there no one here to protect her...
Why no friends in her life to care...
She asked herself these puzzling questions...
No one with whom she could openly share...

All the torment; all the sadness...
All the deep, dark secrets she hid...
She could immediately stop the wretched suffering...
"So long world!" said yet another hopeless kid...

How Much Time Is Left?

Tick tock...
Tick tock...
How much time
Is left on your clock?

What happens when it strikes
On the witching hour...
When the clanging starts
In the old bell tower...

It'll strike some fear
When the Grim Reaper is near...
Will your clock stop ticking
When death starts picking...

Tick tock...
Tick tock...
How much time
Is left on your clock?

You won't hear him coming
Or the song that he's humming...
He'll catch you totally by surprise
With death protruding from his eyes...

Your time is finally up
When the Reaper swings...
It's the end of your life
When the cold alarm rings...

Tick tock...
Tick tock...
Tick tock...
Tick...

With Hollow Eyes

The local priests with their trusting smiles...
Hiding behind the cloth are the pedophiles...
Offering young boys a little wine...
The priest then says "now you're all mine..."

Nothing more than satanic trolls...
Demonic creatures with bankrupt souls...
Nothing more than devils in disguise...
Vicious monsters with hollow eyes...

The lawyers shout "here, take some cash!"
And then the lawsuits go away in a flash...
Then the bishops ship the priests away...
So they can harm yet another day...

The archdiocese erases all the archives...
All that's left are destroyed lives...
Some so broken they fall on knives...
In a secret world where no soul survives...

The Girl In The Lake

Whenever you hear someone is missing...
While fishing on the Lake, somewhere remote...
They mentioned they wouldn't be out too long...
But there's no body in the boat...

After a search for miles and miles...
One that continues late into the night...
But still the body is nowhere to be found...
The search will commence at morning light...

While the family is busy praying...
The neighbors' hope begins to wane...
And then someone always mentions...
The legend of Lake Pontchartrain...

It happened back in the late 60's...
When a little girl went for a swim...
She road her bike off the old Padua Pier...
But was never heard from again...

Her body was never recovered...
The family's closure was never felt...
Her daddy felt especially troubled...
Because he had spanked her earlier with his belt...

It was because the little girl was playing...

That morning in her daddy's shed...
She took one of his tire chains...
And smacked her daddy in his head...

She was scared to death of her dad...
Because he had used that chain to hang her cat...
He chased her back into the house...
Screaming "I'll whip your butt, you little brat!"

She loved her cat so dearly
But her dad was a drunken fool...
He found the cat in his shed
With a dead mouse atop his stool...

He smacked the cat with a backhand
And the cat flew through the air...
He tied a chain around his neck
Until the cat's spirit was no longer there...

She told her dad "I hate you"
As she ran out their home's backdoor...
She rode her bike off the Padua Pier
And was seen again no more...

Now when anyone goes missing
From their boat on Lake Pontchartrain...
Eventually someone will mention
The little girl with the chain...

Even though it was years ago,
And the girl's family has moved away...
The girl with the chain in Lake Pontchartrain
Lives in spirit to this very day...

Image: The Girl in the Sea, Stefan Koidl

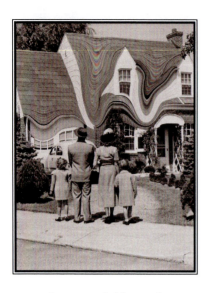

In The Middle Of My Trip

Our house, in the middle of my trip...
Our house, in the middle of my slip...
I keep on trying to get clean...
Daddy's hiding...
Momma's crying...
My pusher's here... he keeps supplying...

I remember when everything was fine...
We were a lovely family; the sun would shine...
I smoked some pot to find cloud nine...

Our house, in the middle of my trip...
Our house, in the middle of my slip...
I keep trying hard to make the scene...
My girlfriend's cheating...
My friends are beating...
My pusher's here and I keep retreating...

I remember when everything was fine...
We were a lovely family; the sun would shine...
I snorted some coke to find cloud nine...

Our house, in the middle of my trip...
Our house, in the middle of my slip...
My dogs are snoring...
My sister's whoring...
My pusher's here and I keep scoring...

I remember when everything was fine...
We were a lovely family; the sun would shine...
I dropped some acid to find cloud nine...

Our house, in the middle of my trip...
Our house, in the middle of my slip...
The cops are raiding...
My life is fading...
Our house is gone and it's so degrading...

I can't remember a thing I said...
It's all gone now and I am dead...

Image: H. Armstrong Roberts

Chapter 7: Self Reflection

The Search For My Serenity

My struggles really started...
When I was just a kid...
Running the streets and getting in trouble...
For everything I did...

I wanted people to like me...
To have friends and be really cool...
But I always felt like a outsider...
Alone, every day after school...

Drinking made me feel popular...
Or more hip when I was a boozer...
But when I wasn't drinker...
I felt like such a loser...

I dreamed of finding happiness...
Fancy cars, girls and wealth...
But the bottle became my way of hiding the pain...
From everyone, including myself...

The more I drank myself...
Into that sad and lonely place...
The more depressed I became...
Longing for something or someone to embrace...

I arrived at a point where I felt...
Nothing but loneliness and pain...
No one wanted anything to do with me...
They treated me with such disdain...

No longer lived a life of happiness...
After losing my family and pride...
Finally looked at myself in the mirror...
Became so empty deep inside...

Realizing I hit my bottom...
Feeling my life was out of control...
The thought of death approached me...
Hopelessness took over my soul...

I found a book about sobriety...
For building a new life with a proven plan...
Written by a guy name Bill W...
Offering a chance to be a better man...

Feeling like I had lost everything...
My world had turned so grim...
I decided to turn over my life...
To the care of God, as I understood Him...

Trying to avoid the happy hour...
Realizing I needed a new me...
Started praying to my Higher Power...
Began the search for my serenity...

Finally some deep soul searching...
A moral inventory of myself...
Finding hundreds of resentments...
Sitting on my emotional shelf...

Admitted to God and my new sponsor...
The exact nature of my wrongs...
Threw out all the old wine glasses...
Stopped singing my old sad songs...

Begged God to remove all my defects...
To place my shortcomings far, far away...
Asked Him for His forgiveness...
To remove my addiction each and every new day...

Made a list of all I had caused harm...
Became willing to make amends to them all...
Followed this 12-step program...
To avoid taking another drunken fall...

Continued to take my personal inventory...
Promptly admitted when I was at fault...
Took responsibility for my own actions...
Put my bad attitude away in a vault...

Now that I have had a spiritual awakening...
The result of this 12-step plan...
Carry this message to other alcoholics...
Try to be a better man...

Understanding my addiction is forever...
Accepting it as a fact of life...
My children have given me a second chance...
My attitude is no longer strife ...

When you're tired of Hotel California...
You think that you can never leave...
The way out is through these 12-steps...
In your Higher Power you must believe...

One day at a time...
Two weeks without the glooms...
Ninety days and you'll be fine...
If you can only make it back to the rooms...

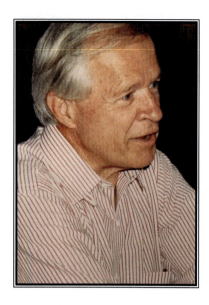

A Tribute To My De

My father passed away today... we knew the time would eventually come... it was a moment we both had planned for... a close relationship ours had truly become...

We spent the last few years... recognizing our love for one another... it was truly a special gift from God... to have this time to spend with each other...

We laughed at all the yelling... and all the punches that we threw... we cherished our fun times together... and winked at the secrets that only we knew...

De was never an Atticus Finch... or a perfect dad by any mean... but he was the best dad a guy like me could ever want... I was so proud of my Marine...

And now he's off to Heaven... to join Madeleine and all the others... to watch over Granne and our family... to watch over the grandchildren, Stephanie and my brothers...

It's time for us to let you go... but your memory will always remain... and I promise to look after Granne... until we see you once again...

I love you, De... thank you for being my Dad... ❤️

My Love For You

I'm not a man of many means...
I'm just a fellow wearing jeans...
But my love for you is real...
If you just give me a chance...
You soon will feel...
My love for you...

I can't buy you no fancy car...
I don't smoke no expensive cigar...
These tears are real coming from my eyes...
The sadness I feel from all your lies...
If you just give me a chance...
You soon will feel...
My love for you...

I can't buy you no diamond ring...
Make you a queen cuz I ain't no king...
My words for you are true...
And all the pain you put me through...
If you just give me a chance...
You soon will feel...
My love for you...

I know I'll never be no poet...
There's no other way for me to show it...
But my love for you is real...
If you just give me a chance...
You soon will feel...
My love for you...

But I'll Endure

The changing of happiness to a deepened sorrow...
Living today as if there's no more tomorrow...
Offering reflections of my deep depression...
Being a parent as a mere concession... but I'll endure...

The daily phone calls and letters that never arrive...
As if my children no longer feel that I'm still alive...
Did I abandon them as I constantly blame myself... am I at fault...

Take me back in my thoughts
To a time of lost happiness...
To a place when my children
Looked into my eyes with unconditional love...

The changing of happiness to a deepened sorrow...
Living today as if there's no tomorrow...
Offering reflections of my deep depression...
Being a parent as a mere concession... but I'll endure...

The photographs that never were taken...
The memories that are now forsaken...
The hugs and kisses that were never shared...
Would life be worth living if my children no longer cared... am I at fault...

Take me back to a time of laughter...
To a place when we ere together...

Take me home to where my children were safe...
When there was a time that I was their protector...

The changing of happiness to a deepened sorrow...
Living today as if there's no more tomorrow...
Offering reflections of my deep depression...
Being a parent as a mere concession... but I'll endure...

Happy Father's Day!

No dad is ever perfect...
Not by any means...
Some dads are super cool...
Some dads make us eat our greens...

Some dads work all the time
And don't get home until late at night...
Some dads have to work two jobs
And don't get home until morning light...

Some dads come home for dinner
And help us with our homework...
Some dads are good with computers
And know about Star Trek and Captain Kirk...

Some dads are good with baseball
And know how to throw a knuckleball...
Some dads are good with pitching tents
And take us camping in the Fall...

Some dads like working on engines
And can teach us to change a spare...
Some dads like to act all silly
But offer kind words if we're in despair...

Sometimes we have a stepdad
Who takes us on fun vacation drives...
Sometimes we have a granddad
Who plays an important role in our lives...

But it's great to have a person
Who helps us grow along the way...
And it's to this important father figure
That we say "Happy Father's Day!"

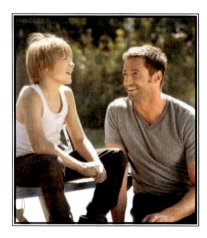

My Letter to Henry

Dear Henry,

I'm glad we were able to meet each other and I hope we can be friends…

Being your mother's boyfriend revolves around one word: Respect…

I want you to know from the start that I respect your mom very, very much…

I also respect you, as her son…

I respect the fact that you are indeed the man of the house, and you are there to make sure that your mom and your sister are safe…

Please know that, in addition to being respectful, I am also a gentleman…

Being a gentleman isn't a personality quirk… it's not something we turn on and off like a switch… it's a choice… it's a lifestyle…

I want you to know that I, as a gentleman, will always treat your mom as the lady that she is…

I'm here to open the door for her as we enter into a building…

I'm here to stand up for her when she arrives late at the table…

I'm here to pull the chair out for her when I take her to a nice restaurant…

I'm here to hold an umbrella over her when it rains…

I'm here to help put on and take off her coat…

I'm here to walk on the outside of the sidewalk so the water doesn't splash her pretty dress…

I'm here to hug her when she needs a hug…

I'm here to hold her hand when her hand needs to be held…

I'm here to tell her she looks pretty when she needs to hear that…

I'm here when she needs a pat on the back when she's done something really good…

I'm here to tell her that dinner tastes great when she's worked so hard in the kitchen…

I'm here to tell her that she looks perfect when she asks me if I think her pants look tight in the back...
I'm here to make her feel safe when you're away...
I'm here to tell her that I really like her when she needs to know that she has a true friend in her life...

These are the things we do for the women in our lives... not just our moms, but for our sisters, and even for our girlfriends...
This is what we do as men... as husbands... as sons... and as boyfriends...
Henry, you have my word, my promise, that I will always treat your mom with respect, and that I will always treat her like the lady that she is...
Thank you for taking the time to hear my thoughts...
Sincerely,
Jeff

A Tribute To The Altobelli Family

They were here one minute and gone the next...
What were your last words to them...
Did you get to say "I love you" or "thank you for being in my life"
Why did God do this to me...

Now you have to make the funeral plans...
Did you know if they wanted a coffin or to be cremated...
Do you have a family plot or a place to spread their ashes...
We never really talked about it...

Will their souls go up to Heaven all together...
Who pays for everything...
Why does Aunt Betty keep telling you it's going to be alright when you know it's never going to be alright...
Momma never really liked Aunt Betty at all...

You just want your parents back...
You want your little sister back, too...
What would momma and daddy want...
When will this nightmare be over...

https://www.waynedupree.com/helicopter-crash-john-altobelli/

You Never Have To Be Alone

I had relatives but I didn't have a family...
I had friends but I didn't have relationships...
I had religion but I didn't have faith...
I had sex but I didn't have intimacy...

I kept asking myself the same questions...
Do you want to feel normal...
Do you want to simply fit in...
And then I finally listened for the answers...

It's up to you to take the first step...
Sitting on the bench is not enough...
Don't merely show up and sit by yourself...
Start off by opening up...
Introduce yourself to the person sitting next to you...

You never have to be alone...
There is always someone who wants to hear your story...

We've all been where you are right now...
We have found an easier way of living and we can show you the path...
Take your time...
We will earn your trust...

Stop looking and start seeing...
Stop thinking and start feeling...

Stop talking and start listening…
Stop taking and start giving…
Stop judging and start accepting…

It's up to you to take the first step…
Sitting on the bench is not enough…
Don't merely show up and sit by yourself…
Start off by opening up…
Introduce yourself to the person sitting next to you…

Raise your hand and say hello…
People around you will reply in kind…
Some people on the outside want you to fail…
The people in AA want you to win…

Stop taking and start giving…
Stop looking and start seeing…
Stop thinking and start feeling…
Stop asking and start receiving…

Take your time…
We will earn your trust…
By listening to others you will soon realize we have a lot in common…
Don't look for the differences…
Look for the similarities…

You are one of us and we will embrace you…
You are finally safe to be who you truly are…
You will never, ever be judged…
We are the family you've always wanted…

Stop doubting and start believing…
Stop fighting and start embracing…
Stop taking and start giving…
Stop thinking and start feeling…

It's up to you to take the first step…
Sitting on the bench is not enough…
Don't merely show up and sit by yourself…
Start off by opening up…

Searching For The Answers

Running down the highway...
Seeking a connection...
Looking for some substance...
Tired of fake affection...

Searching for the answers...
To my many questions...
Trying to put a stop to...
All my sick obsessions...

Tired of all the running...
Lost of all direction...
Craving my solution
Tired of the rejection...

Living in the bottom...
Of an empty bottle...
Always stuck in first gear...
With my broken throttle...

What's the damn solution...
Where's my Higher Power...
Need to find it quickly...
Before my final hour...

Chapter 8:
Cemetery Reflections

The Unknown Soldier

His mother waited in the window until she took her last breath... never receiving the news... never knowing closure... the boy who never returned... the unknown soldier...

The fiancé who cried herself to sleep every night... letters unanswered... days turned to weeks... months turned to years... not knowing whether to remain forever faithful... or to simply move on... the boy who never returned... the unknown soldier...

The dad who was never able to retire... he kept the family business running so that one day his son would have something to return home to... a dad who never lost faith... until he could work no longer... the boy who never returned... the unknown soldier...

The younger brother who lost his idol... a brother he always looked up to... his role model and his protector... feeling too guilty to ever use his catcher's mitt... the boy who never returned... the unknown soldier...

My Baby Blue Angel

He was all I ever hoped for...
He looked exactly like me...
His eyes were blue and sparkling...
He lit the world as bright could be...

He learned to walk and run around...
He learned to talk; what a beautiful sound...
His hair was brown and full of curls...
His momma loved him, so did the girls...

But then one day his sparkle went dim...
His feet stopped running; his hair grew thin...
Our little world he made so bright...
We lost our son late in the night...

From that day on my tears did flow...
Until I realized the sky would glow...
And late at night from the stars above...
My Baby Blue Angel was sending his love...

I See An Angel

I see an angel all cloudy white...
My first intuition is to run in fright...
But should I stay and then I might...
Get a little closer and touch the light...

I see an angel floating high above...
My defensive side says to give it a shove...
But the angel is so pure and white as a dove...
I want to get closer and feel the love...

I see an angel up in the air...
My conflicted side says get out of there...
But all of a sudden I stop and share...
My hand to the angel without despair...

I see an angel up in the sky...
Is her presence a sign to imply...
The end of my life must be nearby...
It's time to tell the world goodbye...

Resting Spirits

Foggy morning
A tranquil place of peace...
Resting spirits
As the blessed souls increase...

When the clouds begin to soften
Eventually to burn off...
It is when these resting spirits
Quietly commence their journey aloft...

These resting spirits ascend
To the Heavens up above...
As they enter a beautiful place
Where there's serenity and love...

No Matter What Class

Ashes to ashes...
Dust to dust...
We all return to the garden...
In that we can trust...

Whether rich or poor...
No matter what class...
At the end of the day...
We end up on our ass...

Mother's Loving Embrace

When life's challenges
Become too heavy to bear...
It's in the cemeteries
That I come to share...
My loving memories
Of having you in my life...
For it's you who takes away
My fears and strife...

Strolling peacefully
Among the silent tombs...
Like resting comfortably
In our mothers' wombs...
Listening to quiet voices
Sharing stories of love...
Making one aware
Of a perfect world above...

Tranquil walks
Among resting souls...
Sharing memories
Of lifetime goals...
Comfortably knowing
That the next chapter begins...
With a warm embrace
From family and friends...

One should never worry
When the end finally arrives...
As Our Lord opens up
His warm and inviting skies...
Knowing that together
We will once again be...
In our mothers' loving embrace
For all the world to see...

Cemetery Ghost

She was a beautiful girl
All dressed in white...
Her eerie calmness
Caused me some fright...

Her hair was combed
Accented with lilies...
To be perfectly honest
She gave me the willies...

She stood there staring
An expression austere...
I wanted to run
But was frozen with fear...

She was there one second
Then gone the next...
I stood for a moment more
Feeling quite perplexed...

In a blink of the eye
She had disappeared...
I got the hell out of there...
The whole thing was weird...

Happy Heavenly Mardi Gras!

We can hear you celebrating Mardi Gras
down here on God's green earth...
"Throw me something mister"
you scream from your heavenly berth...

To all the heavenly angels
celebrating Mardi Gras up above...
We're thinking of you all
with lots of Mardi Gras love...
💜💛💚

Les Amoureux Perdus

Mesdames en deuil ...
Les amoureux perdus ...
Changer des vies pour toujours ...
Un coût incommensurable ...

Plans brisés ...
Plus de rêves ...
Alors que les amoureux nous quittent ...
Du chagrin à notre cœur ...

Lovers Lost

Ladies in mourning...
Lovers lost...
Changing lives forever...
An immeasurable cost...

Shattered plans...
Dreams no more...
As lovers leave us...
Grief to our core...

But Now Is The Time

The time has come
To leave this world...
Rising with angels
Your wings unfurled...

Your job is done
Down here on earth...
Your new mission awaits
Your celestial berth...

As you prepare to watch over
Your loved ones below...
Your Heavenly spirit
Will continue to glow...

Your memory and love
Are forever etched in our heart...
But now is the time
You need to depart...

Image: The Springthorpe Memorial; Boroondara General Cemetery, located in Kew, Victoria, a suburb of Melbourne, Australia

Heading Down The Road

Heading down the road
Going nowhere...
Trying to get away
From my obsessions...
Tired of feeling like
I'm always out there...
Searching for the answers
To my questions...

Just a drunk
Wiping off my last hurl...
Down and out
Seeking just a warm bed...
All alone
Wishing for a nice girl...
With a bosom
On which to place my tired head...

Searching for
That promise of a new life...
Praying for relief
From my confessions...
Heading in the direction
Of going elsewhere...
Open to anyone's good suggestions...

I'd like to find
A nice sober lady...
One who wants to share
My few possessions...
Heading down the road
Leading somewhere...
Hoping to make some big impressions...

Just a drunk
Diving for my last meal...
Down and out
Craving just a warm bed...
All alone
Seeking just a nice field...
With a bed of green grass
On which to place my tired head...

Tell Your Family 'I Love You'

Never put off till tomorrow...
The things you want to do today...
You never know when the hand of death...
Will come to whisk you away...

For all the goals you want to accomplish...
You'll have time over years and months...
You may think you have all the time in the world...
But death is sudden and will come only once...

For all the times you wanted to say "I love you"...
That you allowed to slip quietly by...
It's these times you'll remember regretfully...
As moments gone with the blink of an eye...

So complete your lover's honey do list...
Enjoy the beauty of today...
And tell your family "I love you"...
Before death does take you away...

Image: The Grim Reaper; Montjuic Cemetery; Barcelona, Catalonia, Spain

Ye Young Irish Lads

Where have ye all gone
Ye young Irish lads...
What about all ye children
Who'll no longer have dads...

Why didn't ye stop
And use your head to think...
Instead of ye fightin
Yourself with the drink...

I begged ye to listen...
I begged ye to pause...
All that damn drinkin...
Ye just a lost cause...

Now ye be gone
Leavin ye widow and kid...
What will ye mother-in-law say?
Oh, Heavens forbid!

Image: James A. Sugar

As Their Ship Goes Down

While at war in a dark foreign ocean...
Cannon balls rip in horrendous explosion...
Their boat soon takes on gushing water...
A loss nothing less than a slaughter...

While they are silent, they shout...
Filled with fear, trembling about...
It's their words no one hears
As their prayers fall on deaf ears...

The sailors hold on to each other...
Thinking of their girl, or perhaps their mother...
Hiding a fear for no one to see...
As their ship became one with the unforgiving sea...

Nature's Veil

Ashes to ashes...
Dust to dust...
To deny my love...
Twas so unjust...

You mistreated my gifts...
Like a dog's old bone...
You forsook my attention...
You left me alone...

You escaped my advances...
You eluded my web...
You paid me no respect...
And now you are dead...

You disgraced my honor...
You made me fail...
And now you'll forever wear...
Nature's veil...

The Young Soldiers And Me

Resting peacefully
under the old oak tree...
We were young... we were brave...
We fought valiantly...

We were proud to give our lives
for our beloved country...
This is where you'll find
the young soldiers and me...

Chapter 9: Spirituality and My Relationship With My Higher Power

Personal Essay: My Higher Power

Today, I'm a simple man with simple thoughts, but this wasn't always the case. When I was a child I attended Catholic grammar school. As a young boy, Sister Mary Marcella would tell our class that God was everywhere. I often asked her "but Sister, how can God possibly be everywhere?" And she would answer "because He just is. He's even inside you." To which I would curiously ask, with all the sincerity that a young boy could muster, "but where exactly is He? I don't see Him. How could He possibly be in me?"

Feeling that I was asking my genuine questions out of childish insubordination and defiance, she would order me to the front of the room where, with my back to my fellow classmates, she would sternly demand that I stare straight ahead at a beautiful picture of the Blessed Mother lovingly holding the Christ Child, as Sister Mary would begin to beat me repeatedly with her 36" wooden pointer until I finally cried into submission. While my backside was indeed feeling the pain of these almost daily beatings, my curiosity continued to flourish. I truly wanted to know the answers.

One Sunday evening, I was watching the Disney movie "Pinocchio" with my younger brother Pete, when I misheard Jiminy Cricket tell his lying little puppet friend to simply let your conscience be your God. After hearing these magical words of wisdom, I felt the older brotherly urge to inform Pete that our conscience is actually God inside our bodies. Pete quickly responded in an indignant tone "that's not what he said, stupid. He said conscience be your guide" as I suddenly realized that maybe this is what Sister Marcella was trying to say the whole time. Then I punched Pete as hard as I could, just to remind him who was boss.

It wasn't until later on, when I saw the movie "Animal House" that I fully grasped the concept of real consciousness, and the two sides of my very own personal challenge and daily struggle with my own two sides of good and evil, right and wrong. Now it was finally starting to make sense.

I had to come to terms with why I actually enjoyed the excitement of doing things the wrong way, on purpose, when I knew the difference perfectly well, added to the painful aftermath of my choices. Obviously, that evil enforcer Sister Marcella is still always with me, pointer in hand, just waiting to swing.

I had to know the answers as to why I had to complicate so much of everything in my life. Was it simply a misfiring of my brain? Were my own confused dopamine pathways, which played a major role in the motivational component of reward-motivated behavior or was I truly just a bad person, as Sister Macella and my parents and everyone else always told me throughout my life? Why couldn't I just be normal? Why couldn't I just simply fit in? Why couldn't I simply connect with people?

No matter how hard I tried the results were always the same - loneliness and eventually depression.

I learned very early on, at around the age of twelve, that drinking beer made me feel more relaxed and somehow more popular. This was especially true with older kids, especially with thirteen and fourteen year old girls. The more the girls drank, the friendlier they became with me. This little attraction didn't go unnoticed with the older guys in my neighborhood.

But as every quid pro quo relationship, the moments were always short but sweet, at least until the beer was gone. Because I really didn't have the money, or the maturity, to continue the relationships, they would always dissolve and I would be left alone, yet again.

This would happen over and over again throughout my life, affecting friendships and marriages and jobs and family.

It wasn't until I was 49 years old, divorced and without much to look forward too, other than being an absent father, that I suddenly realized that I needed to look within and somehow find direction. Before I could truly move forward, I had to come to terms with my own conscience and my own moral compass.

It was at this point that I turned within myself to analyze my own inventory of God given tools. I realized I needed balance in my life spiritual, mental and physical balance- and that everything else would simply fall into place.

Today, I have a Higher Power. His name is God and He provides the necessary balance in my life. I sometimes refer to Him as My Heavenly Father or My Sweet Lord, depending upon my moods and my level of consciousness.

My Higher Power also has a feminine side, kind of like a wife. Her name is Mother Nature. Even though I meditate with my Higher Power on a regular basis, I know that His wife really runs all things physical. And never, and I mean never, try to fool Mother Nature.

Together, they help guide me through the spiritual, physical and emotional aspects of my journey. They help me make good, well thought out decisions.

They give me the strength to handle everyday personal challenges, not only with myself, but with my family, friends and strangers.

My thoughts are much less confusing. My life and my needs are much simpler now. I now understand that God is truly everywhere. He is definitely within me.

A Place Where We All Belong

As the sun begins to wake...
And the day begins to break...
Newborn babies commence to stir...
A hungry kitten lets out a purr...

Soon the bacon starts to sizzle...
The sun dries last night's drizzle...
As the day embarks anew...
Coffee and chicory begin to brew...

As the morning paper hits the door...
Little feet scamper across the floor...
Let's go outside into the park...
Children play as parents talk...

Parents and children everywhere...
A peaceful calm that fills the air...
An old stone bridge on which to cross...
Set beneath oaks taken over by moss...

A senior couple holding hands...
Counting blessings and making plans...
A sudden ripple and a breeze...
Brings our worries to their knees...

A mockingbird sings her song...
In a place where we all belong...

Photograph by Monica Dunn Sieja

We Need To Teach Our Children

The children are our future...
We need to teach them all...
We need to show them how to be kind...
To help others if they should fall...

It's the adults from which our kids learn...
We need to teach them to not judge others...
To teach our children to be tolerant...
To accept all our sisters and brothers...

We need to teach them to be sweet...
To be loving to their little friends...
If they should hurt anyone's feelings...
They need to be quick to make amends...

We need to teach them kindness...
To be patient, to share and not yell...
For it's the #1 job of all adults
To teach our children well...

In His Hands

Nature is where men exist in the rawest of conditions... where they fish and they hunt... as one with their environment...

Nature is where men find their voices and their manhood... where they find their redemption... to be part of their natural surroundings...

Nature is where men find their insight and their souls... where they find that true connection with their Higher Power... to be alone with their Creator...

Nature is where men find their voice in silent meditation... to be as one in the hands of Our Heavenly Father... to be honored among the blessed...

Image: The Hunter, Call of the Wild

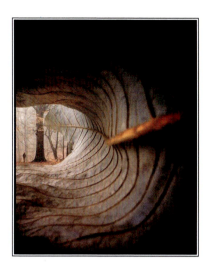

Seeing The Forest Through The Leaves

As I'm walking through the forest...
I begin to roll up both my sleeves...
When I finally arrive at that perfect spot...
To see the forest through the leaves...

As I hear baby sparrows chirping...
In unison with the buzzing of the bees...
It's at this moment when I hear nature's symphony...
The music brings me to my knees...

It's the perfect amount of perfection...
In a lush green forest all around...
With Mother Nature's way of providing...
All the natural treasures we have found...

The very beauty of God's garden...
It's as all the world perceives...
For it's a blessed gift from Heaven...
To see the forest through the leaves...

Photograph: William Smith

The Wanderer

As we wander down that winding road of life...
We make new friends and on occasion, a wife...
But if we don't take time to enjoy good cheer...
Life passes us by as death comes near...

So take the time to smell that sweet rose...
Within a very short time that door will close...
Enjoy your good friends, the wives, the good cheer...
Because the end of the road is closer than you think, dear...

Image: The Wanderer, George Grosz, 1934

The Brotherhood of Manresa

It's that time of the year
When the flowers are in bloom...
As St. Ignatius Loyola summons
The lucky ones to God's Holy Room...

As we retreat to Manresa
From life's daily grind...
It is all in God's Hands
Ourselves we do find...

As St. Ignatius inspires us,
Together, one and all....
He summons us to receive
God's Most Sacred Call...

Dew on the grassy fields
Like a sea of emerald green...
It's a Gift from our Lord
Filled with a love, so serene.

As I'm silently walking
Among the majestic oaks...
Being one with My Father
Lectio Divina needs no coax...

Deep in my Lord's World
As we peacefully pray...
Turning away negative thoughts
as the outside slithers away...

Speaking silently to my Father
on these old bent knees...
Being one in serenity
Among the moss dripped trees...

The Brotherhood of Manresa
is a most spiritual bond...
There's no greater gift from Heaven
If I simply allow Him to respond...

Until next Spring, may all our Thoughts be filled with love...
May God shower us with spirituality
Here on Earth, from Above...

Praying on the Mississippi

As the Mississippi River
Flows along so gracefully...
I feel the power of My Lord
Quickly take hold over me...

Her current is so powerful,
Her rapid water is so warm...
I feel God's love is ever so present,
Blessed thoughts begin to swarm...

The Mississippi has the power
To push boats quickly passed the land...
As I walk peacefully along her banks
And place my worries in God's Hand...

As her fast moving currents steer
The barges down the open river...
I feel God's everlasting presence
An emotion so strong in its deliver...

This magnificent body of water
So vigorous with all its treasure...
It's truly a miraculous blessing
To have God as my almighty measure...

Since the beginning her brown waters
Have flowed rapidly towards the South...
And it's through this mighty river
That God's love will flow past her famous mouth...

God's Nature is so beautiful
Offering peacefulness from above...
As the captains blow their whistles
I'm filled with God's unconditional love...

As I walk along her banks
And gaze at Manresa from the levee...
I feel truly blessed to know my Lord
Is there when my life gets too heavy...

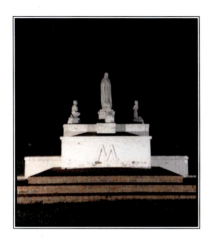

Mother Mary, Pray For Me

When it's early in the morning
And the sun rises over the sea...
Keep me always in your prayers,
Mother Mary, pray for me...

As the sun beats down upon us
And I seek comfort under the old oak tree...
Keep me always in your prayers,
Mother Mary, pray for me...

In the evening when the sun goes down
And the crickets chirp merrily...
Keep me always in your prayers,
Mother Mary, pray for me...

At night time when the stars are sparkling
And the moon shines gleefully...
Keep me always in your prayers,
Mother Mary, pray for me...

As you watch over all Manresa
And you are there for all to see...
Keep me always in your prayers,
Mother Mary, pray for me...

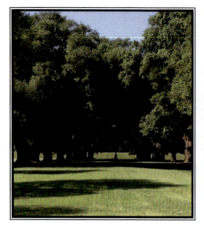 

The Oaks of St. Joseph

Lift me St. Joseph, as you once lifted Jesus.
Share your love, share your strength, share your patience.

Lift me St. Jospeh, as you once lifted Jesus.
Share your humility, as you did when you learned of the blessing from your wife, Mary.

Lift me St. Joseph, as you once lifted Jesus.
Share your humbleness, as you did when God sent his Angel to help you understand your position in life.

Lift me St. Joseph, as you once lifted Jesus.
Share your companionship as you did when you helped Mary raise Jesus, the Son of God.

Lift me St. Joseph, as you once lifted Jesus.
Share your wisdom, as you did when you taught Jesus the tools that were necessary to live here on Earth.

Lift me St. Joseph, as you once lifted Jesus.
Share your understanding, as you did when you let Jesus go off, as a child, to do the work of our Father.

Lift me St. Joseph, as you once lifted Jesus.
Share your brotherhood, as a man, so that I may get the most out of my time here at Manresa.

It's A New Day

Good morning world...
It's a new day...
The Sun has risen...
If we allow ourselves to live in the moment...
If we allow ourselves to receive the gift that nature offers us each and every morning...

It's a new day...
The sky is clear...
The birds are chirping...
If we allow ourselves to leave yesterday behind us...
If we can allow ourselves to receive the gift of a brand new life...

It's a new day...
The neighborhood is quiet...
The smell of breakfast is in the air...
If we allow ourselves to reach out to our family, friends and neighbors and say "good morning"...
If we can allow ourselves to give and receive the gift of love and community...

It's a new day...
The kids are off to school...
Parents are off to work or chores...
The sound of progress is all around us...

If we allow ourselves to be a part of the positive things we all can contribute to each other to make our world a better and safer place...

It's a new day...
Our grandparents are here to give...
If we allow ourselves to truly accept our grandparents as the gifts they offer...
Their love, their wisdom, their experience, their history and their encouragement...
Then we will understand and fully appreciate their importance in our lives...

It's a new day...
The world is a good place...
If we allow ourselves to see all the good that He puts before us...
Then we will be able to truly be a part of this wonderful and loving experience...

It's a new day...
And He has risen...